YORK

Hard Times

Charles Dickens

Note by Neil McEwan

 Longman   ⊕ York Press

Neil McEwan is hereby identified as author of this work in accordance with Section 77 of the Copyright, Designs and Patents Act 1988

YORK PRESS
322 Old Brompton Road, London SW5 9JH

PEARSON EDUCATION LIMITED
Edinburgh Gate, Harlow,
Essex CM20 2JE, United Kingdom
Associated companies, branches and representatives throughout the world

First published 2000
Seventh impression 2005

ISBN 0-582-42449-6

Designed by Vicki Pacey
Phototypeset by Gem Graphics, Trenance, Mawgan Porth, Cornwall
Colour reproduction and film output by Spectrum Colour
Produced by Pearson Education Asia Limited, Hong Kong

CONTENTS

PART ONE

INTRODUCTION

HOW TO STUDY A NOVEL

Studying a novel on your own requires self-discipline and a carefully thought-out work plan in order to be effective.

- You will need to read the novel more than once. Start by reading it quickly for pleasure, then read it slowly and thoroughly.

- On your second reading make detailed notes on the plot, characters and themes of the novel. Further readings will generate new ideas and help you to memorise the details of the story.

- Some of the characters will develop as the plot unfolds. How do your responses towards them change during the course of the novel?

- Think about how the novel is narrated. From whose point of view are events described?

- A novel may or may not present events chronologically: the time-scheme may be a key to its structure and organisation.

- What part do the settings play in the novel?

- Are words, images or incidents repeated so as to give the work a pattern? Do such patterns help you to understand the novel's themes?

- Identify what styles of language are used in the novel.

- What is the effect of the novel's ending? Is the action completed and closed, or left incomplete and open?

- Does the novel present a moral and just world?

- Cite exact sources for all quotations, whether from the text itself or from critical commentaries. Wherever possible find your own examples from the novel to back up your opinions.

- Always express your ideas in your own words.

This York Note offers an introduction to *Hard Times* and cannot substitute for close reading of the text and the study of secondary sources.

'Look how we live', exclaims the power-loom weaver Stephen Blackpool to his employer Josiah Bounderby, and *Hard Times* can be read as a revelation of how people lived in English factory towns at the height of the Industrial Revolution. The fictional Coketown is polluted with smoke and gas, and its mills cripple the workers, some quickly with unprotected machines, and others slowly with unrelieved toil.

'Here I am with my armour on again,' Dickens wrote to a friend, as he began work (9 March 1854). *Hard Times* is a combative novel, hitting out at various targets. Combined with its onslaught on factory conditions and pollution is an attack on unbalanced educational theory and practice, and there is further **satire**, against divorce laws and misguided religious organisations. How these topics are related is one of the critical issues. Many critics see Dickens's prime target as the philosophy of the Industrial Revolution, known as **utilitarianism**.

Utilitarians

Behind the hard times for factory workers was a harsh philosophy, or so the novel alleges. At the climax, the most repellent character, Bitzer, declines to show mercy and asserts that 'the whole social system is a question of self-interest' (p. 287). This was one of the utilitarian principles, on which a system of social and economic laws was constructed to deal with humanity in the mass. Dickens believed that utilitarians were complacent about their ability to understand society through facts and statistics, while disregarding actual human suffering. Such 'a terrible mistake of these days', as he called it (see Literary Background), inspired his satire in the novel, against the selfish, coarse mill-owner Bounderby and even more effectively against the well-meaning intellectual Thomas Gradgrind, the utilitarian whose ideas back Bounderby up.

A fable

This attack was controversial from the first. Dickens used all the arts of his formidable armoury. The novel is shaped like a fable to demonstrate Gradgrind's mistake. We first meet him reforming education, in the new school and in his family, by excluding from education everything except facts and figures. All the rest of human life, he says, is 'Fancy', or nonsense. His eldest daughter and son grow up emotionally and imaginatively stunted, and the consequences shock Gradgrind into humility. He learns wisdom, at the end, from the drunken old circus-master Sleary, whose troupe have **symbolised** the human need for love and imagination that his creed has denied. Admirers are impressed by how the story conveys a whole vision of a crippled industrial society through this simple but powerful scheme. Some critics have always had objections to make.

SOME OBJECTIONS

One problem has been that Dickens was attacking not only the abuses of industrialism but also those who wanted to reform it from within. The utilitarians satirised in Gradgrind were intent on reform. Utility, not tradition, they argued, must be the sole political criterion. Laws, education and government must become more useful and efficient. Through the influence of Jeremy Bentham and other thinkers (see Historical Background, on Utilitarianism), reforms were brought about, although gradually, and too late, Dickens said, for thousands of the ordinary people he claimed to represent.

Socialist critics have always found *Hard Times* both attractive and disappointing. With its passionate concern about human suffering under capitalism, this could have been a classic socialist novel. Yet Dickens attacks all politicians indiscriminately, and presents the trade union members of Coketown as the dupes of a crude mob-orator, and the union as the oppressor of the working-class hero, Stephen Blackpool.

Another difficulty has been that by contrasting 'Fact' and 'Fancy', and passionately attacking 'Fact', Dickens risked seeming to challenge all systematisation and organised knowledge. If so, he was assailing the spirit of his time. He was writing in 1854; the decade began with the Great Exhibition in London in 1851, which displayed thousands of new inventions (including the latest steam engines), and ended with Charles Darwin's *On the Origin of Species*, in 1859. Could the symbol of the circus, and Dickens's imagery drawn from fairy tales and pantomime, really challenge the systematic knowledge of such an age of technology and science?

MODERN VIEWS

Modern critics have mostly decided, for many different reasons, that Dickens has, despite these obstacles, created an extraordinary work of literature. Some historical critics consider that he failed to analyse all the problems, but reflected the struggles and confusions of the first age of industrialism. Feminists have found a new aspect of his tenderness for the oppressed in the novel's portrayal of the plight of women, silenced and excluded in a **patriarchal** society. Linguists have studied the interplay of different voices in the story. Dickens caught a variety of styles of speech, and his targets include tones of voice that betray the falsity of the speakers, Gradgrind stupid with ideas, Bounderby stupid with power, men complacent in their supposed superiority (see Critical History).

All Dickensians enjoy the exuberance of style and imagination. Nothing reads like Dickens. The argument that humanity is imaginative and creative first, and knowing and calculating afterwards (and Dickens was an enthusiast for science), is supported throughout the book by the endless wit and invention of a unique performer, in mid-career and at the height of his powers. There is surprising humour, too, for so grim a story. G.B. Shaw compared Dickens to a mad clown, in his introduction to the novel (see Critical History, on Socialist Views). That is why this fictional account of nineteenth-century people and problems is still read and discussed (and not only in schools) in many parts of the world today.

PART TWO

Summaries & Commentaries

Hard Times *was first published in twenty weekly instalments, in Dickens's magazine* Household Words, *between April and August 1854. The first edition in one volume,* Hard Times for These Times *(1854), is the basis for modern editions. The dedication to Thomas Carlyle was added, and the division into three Books, 'Sowing', 'Reaping' and 'Garnering', was introduced.*

This Note is based on the text of the Penguin Classics edition, edited by Kate Flint (Penguin Books, London, 1995), to which page numbers refer. The Norton Critical Edition, edited by George Ford and Sylvère Monod (Norton, New York, 1990) contains background material, including Dickens's plans and notes for the novel, and correspondence relevant to its composition.

Synopsis

Thomas Gradgrind, a rich man who believes in hard facts and no nonsense, introduces Mr M'Choakumchild, who is to teach facts and drive out 'Fancy' to a class in Gradgrind's model school. Cecilia (Sissy) Jupe, a circus child, cannot define a horse, despite living among horses; a boy called Bitzer recites a definition.

Gradgrind is shocked to find his daughter Louisa and son Tom peeping in at the circus, a bad influence. He takes them home to Stone Lodge where Mr Bounderby, banker, manufacturer and blustery self-made man, is boasting of extraordinary hardships he claims he suffered in early life. The names of two other young Gradgrinds, Adam Smith and Malthus, are an indication of the **utilitarian** philosophy underlying his slogan of 'nothing but facts'. Mr Bounderby kisses pretty, teenaged Louisa, who loathes him.

Gradgrind and Bounderby are leading citizens of Coketown, a dark, polluted industrial town. They visit the circus people, meaning to expel Sissy Jupe from the model school. Sissy, however, has just been abandoned by her father. Gradgrind decides to take and train her in his 'system'. Mr Sleary, the hard-drinking and lisping circus-master, with his philosophy of 'amuthement', offers a sympathetic contrast to Gradgrind and Bounderby, as do the other circus performers.

Mrs Sparsit, a widow, keeps house for Bounderby, a bachelor. Her boasts of past life as a grand lady complement his boasts of early destitution. She is already jealously aware that Bounderby plans to marry Louisa. Under their father's system, Louisa and Tom are emotionally and imaginatively retarded. Sissy's loving heart makes her proof against the Gradgrind system; she cannot understand that nothing counts but hard fact, and that self-interest is the basis of society.

One of Bounderby's hands, Stephen Blackpool, an upright and patient power-loom weaver, consults his employer about divorce. His wife is an alcoholic who torments him; he loves another woman. Bounderby says divorce is too expensive for any but the rich. Stephen considers society 'all a muddle'. Outside the house he meets an old country-woman who venerates Bounderby. That night, in near despair, he is tempted to allow his wife to drink from a bottle of poison. He is saved by the intervention of his beloved Rachael.

Four or five years pass. Sissy and Louisa become attractive young women, and Tom obtains a post in Bounderby's bank. Gradgrind is now a member of Parliament. Wanting to improve his own prospects, Tom urges Louisa, who loves him, to marry Bounderby, thirty years her senior. She consents when her father encourages her to marry him and the marriage takes place. Another year passes. Mrs Sparsit becomes the bank's caretaker, assisted by Bitzer, now a hard-fact believer and the bank sneak.

Mr James Harthouse, a cynical aristocrat hoping for a seat in Parliament, attaches himself to Bounderby. When he learns the truth about Louisa's disastrous marriage from Tom, it amuses him to win her confidence and play with her feelings. They talk about Tom's gambling debts.

One day, Bounderby summons Stephen Blackpool, who has been ostracised by his fellow workers for refusing to join the trade union. Bounderby despises the union and its delegate Slackbridge, a crude demagogue, but Stephen antagonises him with frank support of his fellow-workers, and is dismissed from his job. The old country-woman,

Mrs Pegler, appears again. Tom offers Stephen help, and tells him to wait near the bank every evening until he leaves Coketown. Stephen does so, but no message comes.

Bounderby's bank is robbed. He suspects Stephen (now departed), and Mrs Pegler. Louisa suspects Tom, who refuses to confess to her. Mrs Sparsit stays at Bounderby's, where she spies on Louisa and Harthouse. She daydreams gleefully of Louisa being led astray. Mrs Gradgrind dies, after a life of being browbeaten by her husband.

One night when Bounderby is away, Mrs Sparsit overhears Harthouse declare his love to Louisa. She hurries to tell Bounderby. But Louisa has fled to her father, and told him of her unhappiness. Separated from Bounderby, Louisa befriends Sissy, a happy influence in Gradgrind's home. Gradgrind begins to learn the wisdom of the heart. Armed with simple moral authority, Sissy requires Harthouse to leave Coketown.

Bounderby offers a reward for Stephen's capture, causing Rachael to come forward with Stephen's address; but Stephen cannot be found. Mrs Sparsit catches Mrs Pegler, who turns out to be Bounderby's mother and denies his tales of early neglect; he is only a self-made Humbug.

Rachael and Sissy find Stephen, who has fallen into an uncovered mine-shaft. He condemns the mine-owners, prays for better understanding and asks Gradgrind to clear his name. He dies, with Rachael at his side, confident in his Christian faith.

Humbled by his awareness of Tom's guilt, Gradgrind hopes to help his son escape abroad. Tom is found hiding in the circus. He shows no remorse. Bitzer arrives and seizes Tom. When Gradgrind appeals for mercy, Bitzer repeats his earliest lesson: self-interest is the only principle, in hard fact. Sleary contrives Tom's escape.

Mrs Sparsit is dismissed. The last chapter looks into the future. We see Bounderby dying unlamented, Gradgrind a sadder but wiser man, Rachael in mourning, penitent Tom dying abroad, and Sissy married with children for Louisa to love. Dear reader, the novel ends, let such things be.

BOOK THE FIRST: SOWING

CHAPTER 1 THE ONE THING NEEDFUL

In the new 'model' school: 'Teach nothing but Facts'

An authoritative voice is laying down the law. 'Teach these boys and girls nothing but Facts.' We are given a description of the speaker's square, hard appearance and of how he emphasises 'Fact' by jabbing his square finger on the sleeve of the schoolmaster standing, with one other adult, beside him. The speaker's face and the schoolroom before him look alike: angular and stern. The tiers of children resemble rows of little vessels waiting to be filled, with facts.

> This famous short opening chapter is extremely dramatic. The voice proclaiming the rule of Fact (emphasised by the capital letter) bursts on the reader without any introduction. Gradgrind has not been named yet and nothing has been said about the setting. Another voice, that of the story-teller who describes the speaker, is equally emphatic but otherwise very different. The speaker stresses facts but the narrator is fanciful, turning factual details into **metaphor**: the square forehead is a wall; the eyes are caves; the hair is a plantation of firs; the scalp is the crust of a plum pie, knobbly with facts. Even the repetitions ('square', 'square', 'square') seem to mock the idea of sticking to facts, in a lively way that makes us want to read on. The image of the children as vessels ranged on a factory shelf prepares for later connections between schooling and industry.

> Much of the plot will arise from Gradgrind's determination to teach his own children according to this 'system' of facts and no feelings or imagination. When he boasts about it here on the first page, he is **ironically** unaware of how much sorrow is to be reaped and garnered from this sowing.

> 'Fact' in Gradgrind's usage (with a capital F), and ironically in the narrative, comes to mean more than just information. It stands for a whole view of life, which the novel will condemn.

> **SOWING** the first of many biblical echoes and allusions. See Galatians 6:7, and compare the titles of Books II ('Reaping') and III ('Garnering')

The One Thing Needful see Luke 10:42, where the one thing needful is to hear Christ's teaching

imperial gallons liquid measure in the standard British system

CHAPTER 2 MURDERING THE INNOCENTS

Thomas Gradgrind, a man of facts and figures. How to define a horse. The new teacher, Mr M'Choakumchild

The speaker obsessed with facts and figures is Thomas Gradgrind. He questions two of the children. Cecilia Jupe, who calls herself Sissy but mustn't says Gradgrind, is unable to define a horse properly even though her father works with horses in the circus that has recently come to town. A well-trained boy called Bitzer recites a suitable factual definition. A government official expounds a hard-fact theory of art: carpets and wallpaper must not depict flowers or horses because they are not to be found on floors or walls in reality, and Fact in future is to rule the world. The newly trained teacher, Mr M'Choakumchild, now begins his job of imparting hard facts, and eliminating fancy, if he can.

> This chapter seems to begin with Gradgrind's voice, directed as before straight at the reader, but this time the absence of quotation marks shows he is not actually speaking the words. The narrator is mimicking him: the heavy and smug tone shows how Gradgrind thinks of himself. Dickens's novels often mimic the characters' speech in this manner.
>
> The same beam of sunlight shows up both Sissy's 'lustrous' dark eyes and hair and Bitzer's unusual paleness. These two characters are often to be linked and contrasted.
>
> The chapter title is another of the bitter biblical allusions which imply how far the new doctrine of useful fact and nothing else contradicts the Christian teaching of Faith, Hope and Charity (see Themes, on Religion). Gradgrind's stress on fact, and the third gentleman's theory of art, are products of the **utilitarian** philosophy that is the main target for **satire** throughout the novel (see Themes, on Facts & Figures, and Historical Background, on Utilitarianism).

The name 'M'Choakumchild' is a sign that the author means to have fun with his satirical targets. (For more on names, see Characterisation.) We can now identify the **point of view** as that of an **omniscient narrator**, who sees and knows far more than the characters, and keeps intervening with comments and surprising, often funny comparisons. The writing is exuberant and inventive, in the image of the teacher pouring boiling oil on thieves hidden in jars, for example, meaning that he will try to stifle the children's imaginations.

Murdering the Innocents see Matthew 2:16

galvanizing apparatus Luigi Galvani (1737–98) did experiments with electrical current on animal tissue

the scratch the first boxer unable to stand upright at a line scratched on the ground lost the match

All England a national code for boxing, preceding the Queensberry Rules

Schedule B it provided a programme for teacher-training, widely criticised for overemphasis on rote-learning of the kind satirised in Bitzer's definition of a horse

Morgiana in the Forty Thieves a slave-girl in the tale of Ali Baba and the Forty Thieves, in the *Arabian Nights*, who killed the thieves by pouring boiling oil on them while they were hiding in large jars

CHAPTER 3 A LOOPHOLE

Two of Gradgrind's children are degrading their minds by peeping at the circus

Gradgrind's five children are all suffering under his system of education, all facts and figures, with no 'nonsense' about feelings or imagination. Walking home to his big square house, Stone Lodge, Gradgrind is horrified to find his teenaged daughter Louisa and her younger brother Tom peeping in at the back of the circus, a **symbol** of fancy and folly. 'What would Mr Bounderby say?' he asks, but fails to notice how this name distresses Louisa.

Sleary's Circus, with its typical nineteenth-century blend of horse-riding and pantomime, is an obvious contrast to the 'model' school: it attracts children.

Gradgrind is obsessed with figures as well as facts, and the **imagery** begins to make fun of tables and statistics. Stone Lodge looks like a ledger passed by the accountant: 'a calculated, cast up, balanced, and proved house'. In this way, figures link education with commerce and manufacturing, also controlled by the hard-fact mentality.

The feeling that Gradgrind deserves respect for teaching his son and daughter ('his metallurgical Louisa') science and technology, and for having all the latest inventions, including lifts, in his house, may cause us to react against some of Dickens's **satire**. He replied to such criticism by saying he attacked Gradgrind's fact-and-nothing-else philosophy, taken to such an extreme that children were treated like machines. Thomas is carted off home 'like a machine' (see Themes, on Facts & Figures).

Twinkle, twinkle, little star from a nursery rhyme; the cow with a crumpled horn is from another

Professor Owen Sir Richard Owen (1804–92), zoologist and anatomist

Great Bear … Charles's Wain names for the constellation of Ursa Major, also called the Plough

Peter Piper (tongue-twister), 'Peter Piper picked a peck of pickled pepper'

in an ecclesiastical niche of early Gothic architecture as though in a recess in a medieval church

Signor Jupe English entertainers often used Italian names or titles

William Button this and the Tyrolean Flower Act were current circus acts in 1854 (see Historical Background, on Circuses)

House of Correction prison and reformatory

Mrs Grundy a legendary prude

CHAPTER 4 MR BOUNDERBY

> **The culprits taken home. Self-made bully Bounderby and feeble Mrs Gradgrind. Sissy Jupe must be expelled. Louisa, Bounderby's 'pet'**

Mr Bounderby is lecturing Mrs Gradgrind, in her drawing room, on his own merits. He is a big, loud man who is boasting, with lots of vivid detail, about the incredible early hardships he claims he suffered after his mother abandoned him in infancy. Since then he has risen to eminence as a banker and manufacturer, apparently through his own efforts. Mrs Gradgrind is 'a little, thin, white, pink-eyed bundle of shawls, of surpassing feebleness, mental and bodily' (p. 22), who offers no resistance to Bounderby's bullying talk. When Gradgrind comes home with the 'culprits', Bounderby eyes Louisa. Gradgrind and Bounderby agree that the circus is as bad an influence as literature, and decide to remove the circus-child, Sissy Jupe, from the model-school. Before they set off to see her father, Bounderby kisses Louisa, who afterwards tells Tom how much she detests it.

> Bounderby is a satirical portrait of the type of factory owner who boasted of early struggles in order to justify his wealth and his workers' poverty. Mrs Gradgrind has been ground in her husband's scientific mill. There are examples here of Dickens's recurring tags. Some are labels for characters: Bounderby is 'the Bully of humility' (p. 21). Others are characteristic phrases, such as Mrs Gradgrind's 'go and be somethingological' (p. 24). Readers new to Dickens may be surprised by the dramatic impact of Bounderby and Mrs Gradgrind. The fluency and vitality of Bounderby's talk imparts tremendous energy. But Mrs Gradgrind's listlessness has a strange force of its own. We get an alarming sense of her disordered mind. Gradgrind has driven all 'nonsense' out of her head, and facts will not stick there. Crushed by her domineering husband, she is of special interest to feminist critics (see Themes, on Women's Lives, and Critical History, on Feminist Criticism).

> The names of Gradgrind's two younger children, Adam Smith and Malthus, connect him with **utilitarianism** and its doctrines of self-interest and laissez-faire (French: 'leave alone'), attacked throughout the novel. Gradgrind's 'Fact' comes to stand for this whole body of theory (see Themes, on Facts & Figures, and Historical Background, on Utilitarianism).

transparency a translucent print to be lighted up

St Giles's a poor area of London

Adam Smith (1723–90) economist and author of *The Wealth of Nations*. He was credited with the principle of laissez-faire, advocating minimum government interference in commerce and industry

Malthus Thomas Malthus (1766–1864), writer on the dangers of population growth, which he was the first to analyse scientifically

pipe-clay fine white clay for modelling, and for whitening clothes

CHAPTER 5 THE KEY-NOTE

Coketown, city of smoke and endless labour. Gradgrind and Bounderby meet Sissy Jupe

The key-note is Coketown, a blackened and polluted industrial town, full of factories, mills and chapels, evocatively described. We are told that the factory owners ruthlessly enforce the hard facts of industrial life. Coketown is a town for work and nothing else. Like the Gradgrind children, the workers of Coketown desperately need an occasional holiday.

Gradgrind and Bounderby meet Sissy Jupe (and briefly Bitzer). She is carrying a bottle of 'nine oils' for her father's bruises and sprains from the ring. They reach the public house where the circus people, known as 'strollers' or 'horse-riders', are staying.

> The story-teller presides, appealing to us to share his view of Coketown and judgements on it. The description uses realistic details of pollution and monotony, and also creates a nightmare-like vision. As in previous chapters, imagination asserts itself by transforming the physical details of the town that is 'fact, fact, fact' (p. 29) into **images**: columns of smoke become coiling serpents and a steam-engine piston continually going up and down is 'like the head of an elephant in a state of melancholy madness' (p. 28). These two 'key-note' images are to be repeated like a refrain throughout the novel (see Textual Analysis, Text 1, and Imagery & Symbolism).

> Fact also rules the religious life of Coketown. The chapels of the eighteen religious denominations all look like warehouses, and all fail in their Christian duty to minister to the workers. The words ending this paragraph (p. 29), 'world without end, Amen', echo the Book of Common Prayer of the Church of England. Mimicking religious language is a frequent **ironical** device (see Themes, on Religion, and Language & Style).

lying-in hospital maternity hospital
Teetotal Society Dickens strongly opposed Sabbatarian and Teetotal
societies which interfered with the limited leisure time of working people
(see Themes, on Religion).

CHAPTER 6 SLEARY'S HORSEMANSHIP

**Signor Jupe has disappeared. Gradgrind takes charge of
Sissy, to train her in his system. Mr Sleary, circus-master,
explains his philosophy of amusement**

Mr Jupe cannot be found at the Pegasus's Arms, where the strollers
are staying. Gradgrind and Bounderby are joined by two other
performers, Mr E.W.B. Childers, and an undersized boy called
Master Kidderminster (or 'Cupid', from his role in the ring). Using many
special circus terms in their speech, they explain that Jupe has been doing
badly in his act and may have absconded, taking his performing dog
Merrylegs but deserting Sissy. Other circus people assemble, headed by
Mr Sleary. When Bounderby roughly states the hard facts of the situation
to the unhappy Sissy, they show their disapproval. Remembering that her
father wanted her to be educated, Sissy accepts Gradgrind's offer to take
charge of her, even though the circus people, a close community, would
be glad to keep her. Mr Sleary makes a speech in his characteristic
asthmatic lisp, setting out his philosophy: life is not all work; people must
be 'amuthed'.

The circus is contrasted to Coketown in various ways. In
Coketown, 'the relations of master and man all fact' (p. 29), but the
circus is a place of affection and solidarity where Sleary is first
among equals. Horses and acrobats dominate our impressions of
the circus, in contrast to machines in Coketown. The pantomime
acts in Sleary's repertoire link the circus with the theatre, and so
bring the world of the arts within his philosophy of amusement, in
contrast to the mechanical and heartless society described in the
previous chapter, where culture seems to have broken down. Some
critics point out that the difference between the circus people
and settled industrial society is reinforced by the circus jargon,
which Bounderby finds as puzzling as another language. Tones

of voice are also contrasted in this scene. Bounderby is rough and unfeeling. Although husky and drink-sodden, Sleary speaks cogently, and far more tenderly than Bounderby or Gradgrind. His use of the term 'cackler' for a performer with a speaking part (such as a clown's patter) prepares for his very effective 'cackling' at the end of Book III Chapter 8 (see Language & Style).

Pegasus (Greek mythology) a winged horse

Booth a portable wooden structure; large tents for circuses were adopted later

Newmarket coat a close-fitting rider's coat

Contaur (Greek mythology) half horse and (top) half man

bismuth a white cosmetic

ochre gold, or money

garters hoops

banners streamers

bespeak a private performance

goosed hissed

Lord Harry the devil

Thquire Squire, here a nondeferential style of address

morrithed morrised, run away

pound it put a pound on it, or bet

pursy asthmatic

CHAPTER 7 MRS SPARSIT

Self-made Bounderby is proud of his housekeeper, Mrs Sparsit, a high-born lady

Mrs Sparsit, a widow, keeps house for Mr Bounderby, a bachelor. Bounderby delights in her talk of upper-class relations, including a Lady Scadgers, and the luxury of her past life, and he stresses how she has come down in the world as he has risen. He talks of this to Sissy, who lodges briefly with him until Gradgrind, accompanied by Louisa, takes her home to be trained by his system and attend on his wife. Gradgrind is shocked to learn that Sissy used to read fairy tales with her father. He means to cure her of all such nonsense.

Mrs Sparsit is another character with an immediate dramatic impact. Facial expressions make her comic and sinister, as she raises her Roman nose, as proud as Coriolanus, and contracts her black eyebrows over her teacup. So do her tones of voice: her way of saying 'sir' honours herself more than her master. Her jealousy of Louisa, eventually an obsession, begins in this scene, where Bounderby speaks possessively of Louisa as 'the little puss' (p. 50). His words about taking Tom 'under his wing' in the same passage, also prepare for future developments. It is to improve his credit with Bounderby that Tom later urges Louisa to marry him. There is an **irony** in the point that, under Bounderby's wing, Tom is going to rob his bank.

Bounderby and Gradgrind are contrasted here. Bounderby has no sympathy for Sissy. However misguided the system by which Gradgrind plans to 'train' her, he means well. He cannot guess what a failure his training will be, or how he will come to depend on the very qualities of imagination and sympathy in Sissy which, ironically, he now wants to suppress.

car carriage
blind hookey a card game
Hebrew monetary transactions loans at high interest
Insolvent Debtors Court court for bankrupts, where Dickens's father had appeared in 1824
Calais bankrupts often took refuge from English law, which imprisoned debtors, in this northern French port
Coriolanian broken, Roman nose, like that of the arrogant hero of Shakespeare's *Coriolanus*
Magna Charta ... Bill of Rights historical references typical of patriotic speeches of the time
Princes and Lords ... as a breath has made from 'The Deserted Village' (1770), by Oliver Goldsmith (1730–74), lines 53–4
Italian Opera theatre in Haymarket, London
link a hand-held torch
May Fair London's most fashionable and expensive district
Fairies ... the Dwarf ... the Hunchback ... the Genies in the *Arabian Nights*

CHAPTER 8 NEVER WONDER

The Gradgrind system, its nature and effects; Louisa wonders before the fire; Tom grows cunning

The sense of wonder is to be stamped out in young and old. Louisa cannot help wondering about the future. Tom wants to use his sister's influence with Bounderby.

The key-note linking Gradgrind's philosophy and Coketown's heartlessness is struck again, with the phrase 'Never wonder'. Gradgrind has taught Louisa never to do so, and Mr and Mrs M'Choakumchild stamp out the children's sense of wonder in the model-school. Gradgrind is afraid the workers may be reading literature in Coketown's library. Louisa and Tom are unhappy under their father's system, which is already stunting their imaginations and feelings. Louisa sits staring at the fire. Tom grows selfish. He is already planning to use Louisa to help him manage Bounderby, who offers an escape from the restrictions of home. Looking into the flames, Louisa wonders aloud about their future, until her mother reminds her that wonder is forbidden. If Mr Gradgrind heard, his wife would 'never hear the last of it' (p. 59), her favourite, often recurring phrase.

> Fire is one of the **symbols**, linked with smoke, in the novel's vision of Coketown and in its characterisation. Fire comes to signify wonder and passion, in Louisa's mind, and this scene prepares for the dramatic and moving moment when she says 'Fire bursts out, father!' (p. 103) at the climax of one of the novel's most impressive scenes, in Book I Chapter 15 (see Textual Analysis, Text 2).

> The appearance of Mrs Gradgrind, unloved and unloving, at the end of the chapter emphasises how heartless a home this factual regime has produced. Louisa's love for Tom is all that has survived. Later scenes will imply that her affection is unbalanced. His judgement on himself, 'a Donkey' (p. 56), is truer than he knows.

library free public libraries were a new feature of industrial towns in the 1850s. Dickens was a keen supporter

De Foe Daniel Defoe (1660–1731), author of *Robinson Crusoe* (1719), one of Dickens's favourite books

Euclid Greek mathematician who laid the foundations of geometry

Goldsmith Oliver Goldsmith, author of *The Vicar of Wakefield* (1766)

Cocker Edward Cocker (1631–75) wrote an arithmetic textbook for schools; it was used for so long that his name became proverbial. Dickens considered 'According to Cocker' as a possible title for the novel

CHAPTER 9 SISSY'S PROGRESS

Why Sissy is slow to learn; and how to look after No. 1

Sissy is sure her father still loves her and hopes for his return. Mr Gradgrind shows no sympathy with such nonsense. She makes little progress at school. She cares more about human suffering than about statistics, and so she cannot see the point of Mr M'Choakumchild's questions. Asked for the basic principle of Political Economics, she says, 'To do unto others as I would they should do unto me', which is the opposite of the expected answer (self-interest). She cannot calculate the percentage of people involved in disasters because she sympathises with the victims too much to do the sums. She tells Louisa how stupid she is. Louisa is interested in Sissy's memories of the circus and her loving father and story books. Meanwhile Tom wants his sister to be nice to Mr Bounderby, for his sake. Mrs Gradgrind worries over all the things she is never to hear the last of, but her husband's eye, a 'wintry piece of fact' (p. 67), silences her.

> The **satire** is directed remorselessly at several related targets. The targets in this chapter are self-interest and 'calculation'. Tom calculates mostly on behalf of 'number one' (p. 67), that is to say, himself. **Ironically**, his growing selfishness is logically consistent with his father's **utilitarian** theory. One of its principles is that human affairs can be measured in statistical tables (hence the stress on averages and percentages in the teaching), and another that the fundamental principle in economics is self-interest (this one strongly supported by Bounderby, to whom Tom is beginning to attach himself).
>
> Emotions and sympathies have no place in this theory. Sissy's failure, while living by love, to make progress at Gradgrind's school, stresses ironically the wrongness of its teaching. Some may hear an

echo of *Pilgrim's Progress* in the chapter title, since this **allegory** of the Christian life, by John Bunyan (1628–88), is a book Dickens often mentions. Sissy's presence in Gradgrind's house has brought circus memories into the stronghold of hard fact, where they function as secret agents: "'Father's a;" Sissy whispered the awful word; "a clown'" (p. 64).

Actuary a recorder of court proceedings

To do unto others ... unto me see Matthew 7:12

blue book parliamentary reports, full of statistics, bound in blue

the Sultan ... her head cut off in the *Arabian Nights*, Scheherazade postpones execution by telling her husband the Sultan 1,001 stories on successive nights

CHAPTER 10 STEPHEN BLACKPOOL

Two Coketown 'Hands', Stephen and Rachael, are old friends; Stephen's alcoholic wife returns to torment him

Stephen Blackpool, 'Old Stephen', lives deep in the labyrinth of narrow smoky streets in working-class Coketown. He is a power-loom weaver of forty, though his stoop and grey hair make him look older, and 'a man of perfect integrity' (p. 69).

Work is over and the gas lights, which by day make the factories look through the smoke like fairy palaces, have been turned off. Stephen seeks his 'old friend' Rachael. A married man, but separated from his alcoholic wife for five years, Stephen loves Rachael. He accepts her judgement that it is better for them not to be too often together, because her word is his law. At home, he finds that his wife has returned. As usual she taunts, shames and robs him.

This chapter prepares for the attack on the divorce laws in the next. Stephen's wife is merciless; he is usually patient. Some critics complain that the virtuous qualities of Stephen and Rachael, which we now begin to observe, are unrealistic and sentimental. There are various points to consider. Victorian conventions meant that Mrs Blackpool's sexual promiscuity could only be hinted at in a sort of in code, 'fouler ... in her moral infamy' (p. 72), and also that Stephen and Rachael had to be obviously innocent of any 'misconduct'. Dickens, moreover, wanted to show a 'perfect integrity' in working people. He did so partly for the sake of the novel's attack on factory owners and their intellectual backers, and partly because he believed such integrity really existed. Their dialect helps preserve the characters' dignity. It is not a perfect rendering of Lancashire speech, but it captures a rhythm and tone distinct from those of Bounderby and Gradgrind. It sounds like good ordinary native English, unlike the loud pomposity and inflated rhetoric of better-educated characters (see Language & Style).

black ladder a slide used by undertakers to lower coffins from upper rooms
Titanic (Greek mythology) the Titans were a race of gods

CHAPTER 11 NO WAY OUT

Bounderby explains to Stephen that divorce is only for the rich

The working day begins before daybreak; the gas lights go on and bells summon the workers. Soon the serpents of smoke in the sky and steam engines that look like 'melancholy-mad elephants' will be visible again. The narrator contrasts the mechanical power of the mill and the incalculable mystery in every working man. Stephen works at his loom until noon, when he calls on his employer Bounderby, at lunch in his big brick house, with Mrs Sparsit in attendance. This lady appears shocked by Stephen's enquiry: how can he end his nineteen-year-old unhappy marriage? He seems to be questioning the law and religion of the land, saying the divorce laws lead to violence and murder. Bounderby tells him that divorce is too expensive for the poor. Stephen comes to his usual verdict on society: 'tis a muddle', and Bounderby, who had thought him a good uncomplaining workman before, now fears that 'a mischievous stranger' (political agitator) has got at him. He has shocked a born lady, and shown traces of the 'turtle soup, and venison and a gold spoon' – Bounderby's often-repeated formula for the unreasonable aspirations of his workers (p. 80).

Bounderby and his fellow-masters favour the term 'Hand' for a worker, and it appears several times in this scene. A submissive man like Stephen is 'a steady Hand', but his bow is not servile: 'these

Hands will never do that! Lord bless you, sir, you'll never catch them at that' – another example of the narrator's mimicking of a character's speech (p. 75). This feature of Bounderby's language reflects his thinking, it is implied. There is a **metonymic** reduction of people to parts. Stressing 'Hands' reinforces the novel's attack on theorists who treat people as units, and so enable men like Bounderby to take advantage of it.

Stephen's reference to crimes of violence in unhappy marriages prepares for the scene of the poison bottle in Chapter 13. Bounderby's warning, that Stephen will get into a worse muddle one of these days, prepares for their next scene together, when Stephen rashly contradicts Bounderby on the subject of 'mischievous strangers', in Book II Chapter 4.

It is **ironic** that Bounderby should stress the sanctity of marriage; he will later be quick to repudiate Louisa.

submissive to the curse of all that tribe the serpent is cursed by God in Genesis 3:14

netting a form of needlework

stirrup in netting, threads were wound about one foot

dree long and dull

played old Gooseberry played the devil

brigg bridge

hottering raging

fair faw a' them good luck to them

'Sizes Assizes, periodic court sittings under judges

Doctors' Commons a legal institution in London that dealt with marriage and divorce (see Historical Background, on Divorce)

a thousand ... pound a weaver earned less than £100 a year

not your piece-work Stephen is paid by the piece, not by the hour

CHAPTER 12 THE OLD WOMAN

Stephen meets an old woman who reveres Bounderby

An old country-woman stops Stephen when he leaves Bounderby's house. She asks about 'that gentleman', meaning Bounderby. Did he look well? She and Stephen walk together. She says she comes into Coketown once a year to take a look at that gentleman; this year he has not come out, so Stephen's report will have to do. She thinks it must be wonderful to work for that gentleman. Later Stephen sees her gazing proudly at Bounderby's mill.

> Even if we cannot guess who she is, the old woman seems a possible threat to Bounderby's independence of human ties. The plot links all the characters, implying that life binds us all together, but selfish or misguided characters want to rely only on themselves. Bounderby denies that anyone ever helped him, but perhaps he is not as 'self-made' as he claims. The old woman is another character who acts out her role with dramatic speeches and gestures, kissing Stephen's hand, for example, when she hears he has worked for Bounderby for twelve years.

abate the raging of the sea see Matthew 8:23, where Jesus stills the storm at sea

Hummobee humming-bee

Parliamentary Parliament had required railway companies to provide one cheap train a day on each line

Towers of Babel see Genesis 11:1–9

CHAPTER 13 RACHAEL

Stephen is tempted to let his wife die; Rachael saves them both

On the way home, Stephen broods about the unfairness of death. Why should it take loved wives and spare worthless ones? At home he finds Rachael at the bedside of his wife, who is in an alcoholic coma. A storm shakes the house; wrapped in thought, Stephen had not noticed it outside. Rachael dresses Mrs Blackpool's self-inflicted injuries with a cloth soaked in liquid from a bottle marked with a warning: it is poison to drink. This bottle frightens Stephen. After sleeping, and dreaming of his own damnation (execution before an altar and a vast crowd of witnesses), he wakes and sees his wife about to drink the poison. He half-prays that Rachael will wake. She wakes, and disposes of the bottle in time to save Mrs Blackpool's life, and, he believes, Stephen's soul, because he might not have been willing to stop his wife drinking the poison. He tells Rachael that her image will always come to mind and keep him from angry thoughts in future.

Stephen's dream, narrated in detail, is a striking example of the omniscient or godlike **point of view**

The scene in Book II Chapter 4 where Stephen stands before his fellow-workers may recall the dream, where he is condemned by a vast crowd. The supernatural realm is vividly present in Stephen's mind in this chapter. He sees the light behind Rachael's head as a halo. His pledge to Rachael, to restrain his anger for her sake, is sacred and prepares for the promise he refers to when he explains why he cannot join the trade union. This promise would have been clearer if Dickens had not cancelled a passage which appears in his manuscript after 'a' the muddle cleared awa" (p. 92). Here he referred to Rachael's sister's death in a factory accident and spoke indignantly about the owners' neglect of safety precautions in factories. Rachael begged him to leave ('let be') such matters alone, and he said 'I pass my promise'. The cancelled lines are included in the end-notes (p. 309) to the Penguin edition (see Factory Accidents, in Historical Background).

Let him who ... stone at her Jesus says these words, of the woman taken in adultery, John 8:1–11

there is a deep gulf set see Luke 16:26, for the gulf between the rich man Dives in Hell and the poor man Lazarus in Heaven

saved my soul alive the words are from Ezekiel 18:27; the quotation shows Stephen's close knowledge of the Bible

CHAPTER 14 THE GREAT MANUFACTURER

> **Time turns out Sissy, Louisa and Tom as young adults. A clerk in Bounderby's bank, Tom wants Louisa to marry the banker**

Some years go by. The changes are presented as the work of Time, **personified** as the greatest of Coketown's manufacturers. Sissy leaves school. Although his system has failed in her case, Gradgrind can sense her goodness, which puzzles him. Time has made him Member of Parliament for Coketown. Time has turned Tom into a young man, now employed in Bounderby's bank, and Louisa into an attractive young woman. On the eve of her appointment to see her father for a serious talk, as she sits watching the sparks and ashes in the fireplace, Tom asks her to agree to 'I know what', for the sake of his future in the bank. He means, agree to marry Bounderby. Watching the distant furnaces of Coketown, Louisa wonders what the future will bring; Time's factory, however, 'is a secret place' (p. 98).

> The image of Time as a manufacturer adds to the novel's vision of Coketown as a place where manufacturing is the only purpose of life, and where people are thought of as units, as though they were machine parts or products. Time is said to have 'turned out' Tom a foot taller, and 'passed Sissy onward in his mill, and worked her up into a very pretty article indeed' (p. 94). We are reminded of the wonder and mystery of time in human life in the lines about the secret factory and silent Hands at the end of the chapter, and also in the fire imagery of sparks and ashes (see Textual Analysis, Text 2, and Imagery & Symbolism).

> The contempt expressed for Parliament ('deaf ... dumb ... dead honourable gentlemen', p. 96) becomes even more pronounced in later passages (see Language & Style).

parliamentary return   an official report, full of facts and figures

CHAPTER 15   FATHER AND DAUGHTER

Father tells daughter to use her head and forget her heart. Louisa agrees to marry Bounderby

A 'deadly-statistical clock' ticks in Gradgrind's study (p. 99), a severe and sinister room, full of government 'blue books'. Here social questions are to be 'cast up' and settled, like accounts, says the narrator (p. 99). Gradgrind receives Louis a here and informs her of Bounderby's proposal of marriage. When she asks if he thinks she loves Bounderby, he dismisses sentiment as irrelevant and tells her to concentrate on the facts. Bounderby is fifty and she is twenty, so there is some difference of age, which statistics show is not unusual. Gradgrind expects her to think rationally, free from 'nonsense'. For one moment Louisa feels 'impelled to throw herself on his breast' and reveal 'the pent-up confidences of her heart'. But Gradgrind cannot sense how she feels. Watching the smoke from the factory chimneys from the window, Louisa exclaims that while the scene by day is covered in smoke, at night 'Fire bursts out'. Gradgrind cannot imagine what she means by that. She now consents to the marriage. Her father congratulates her. When Mrs Gradgrind hears the news she is baffled about what to call her son-in-law. She cannot use his surname now, and she loathes the name Josiah. Sissy gives Louisa one look of pity, which Louisa will be very slow to forgive.

This is a crucial stage in the novel's design. The title 'Father and Daughter' draws attention to the **ironic** point that his fatherly guidance and her dutiful obedience have culminated in this unnatural scene. It is the climax of Gradgrind's experiment with Louisa's upbringing, and of her lifelong suppression of 'sentiment'. Her only protest comes in the **image** of fire bursting out, like a Coketown furnace in the night. Gradgrind has no notion of fire as a **symbol** of forces that cannot be measured or predicted, including passion and revolt. There are many signs that he is genuinely proud of her, finally asking for a kiss. We may reflect that Gradgrind has always acted with the best intentions, unlike Bounderby who thinks only of himself. This chapter asserts that he is wrong, bringing all the **satire** of the story so far to bear on this confrontation, and for once explicitly naming the pernicious philosophy to blame, to be found in his 'unbending, utilitarian, matter-of-fact face' (p. 102), which hardens Louisa again when she is on the brink of showing her feelings (see Textual Analysis, Text 2).

Mrs Gradgrind, unable to address Bounderby properly, is one of several characters who have trouble with others' names (see Characterisation, and Textual Analysis, Text 3).

Blue Beard he keeps his murdered wives' bodies in a secret room, another of the novel's many allusions to fairy stories
the Calmucks of Tartary a Mongolian nomadic tribe; very far removed from Louisa's situation
the last trumpet to be sounded on Judgement Day; see Revelation 11:15

CHAPTER 16 HUSBAND AND WIFE

Pitying Bounderby, Mrs Sparsit withdraws to a job at the bank. The wedding takes place, with no nonsense

Bounderby buys smelling salts before he breaks the news of his engagement to Mrs Sparsit, expecting her to faint with shock in a grand ladylike manner, but she disappoints him. Indeed, she pities him. They arrange that Mrs Sparsit will become a superior sort of janitor at the bank. Eight weeks are allowed for wedding preparations. Love assumes 'a manufacturing aspect', as presents and cake and financial settlements are all assembled (p. 110). The wedding takes place, with no nonsense. Bounderby boasts, beginning as always, 'I am Josiah Bounderby of Coketown' (p. 110). Tom whispers his thanks to Louisa before they leave for their honeymoon in the textile city of Lyons, where Bounderby means to look into French manufacturing.

> Dickens obviously enjoyed writing about Bounderby, and sometimes makes him seem a pure figure of fun, rather than a target for satire. This happens with the smelling salts in this chapter: 'By George!' said Mr Bounderby, 'if she takes it in the fainting way, I'll have the skin off her nose at all events' (p. 106). He says this to himself, and some readers may share his private satisfaction at the prospect of taking revenge at last on the Sparsit nose. There is another moment of pure fun when he approaches Mrs Sparsit, checking with his hand that the cork of the smelling-salts bottle is ready for use (see Textual Analysis, Text 3).

> The insistence on matter-of-fact plain speaking, in Bounderby's wedding speech, links him with Gradgrind. They both stick to a simple notion of 'fact', and a one-to-one correspondence between language and things, while the novel's language is full of surprises (see Language & Style).

apartments rooms
light porter not required to carry heavy objects
breakfast Victorian weddings were usually held in the morning
bottoms holds of ships

the calculating boy George Bidder (1806–78), a prodigy; his name is
recalled in 'Bitzer'
Lyons a silk-manufacturing centre, and a town disliked by Dickens

Book the second: reaping

chapter 1 effects in the bank

Coketown on a sunny day, even more horrible. Bitzer and Mrs Sparsit guard the bank and share unsentimental opinions. A stranger calls

We are shown Coketown on a sunny day, suffocatingly hot and polluted
by smoke and oil. There is an account of how the factory-owners resist
expensive reforms intended to benefit their Hands.

A year has gone by. Out of business hours, Mrs Sparsit presides in
the bank, assisted by Bitzer, the light-duty porter and bank spy. Bitzer
and she agree about the fact that the trade union ought to be crushed.
Bitzer cannot understand why working people want amusements, or
marry when they cannot afford it. They agree that Tom is the least
satisfactory of the clerks, and a gambler, helped with money by his sister.
A strange gentleman calls, looking for Bounderby. Mrs Sparsit is
impressed by his looks and languidly gentlemanlike manner. He is
interested to hear her account of Mrs Bounderby. After he has gone,
Mrs Sparsit exclaims aloud to herself on what a fool Bounderby has
been.

The key-note Coketown is sounded again at the opening of Book
the Second, with a renewed attack on factory-owners, including a
reference to negligence as a cause of accidents ('chopping people up
with their machinery', p. 115), and a series of images of ugliness and
pollution which outwardly correspond to the inhumanity of the
Coketown bosses. Mention of the Home Secretary (p. 116) refers
to Lord Palmerston (1784–1865), who gave in to a delegation of
owners protesting against safety measures in factories, in February
1854.

More links are formed among characters – Bitzer, Mrs Sparsit,
Harthouse (the strange gentleman) – that will be useful for the plot

and also reaffirm Dickens's point that in spite of class divisions everyone is connected with everyone else. Bitzer is to be developed as another target for satire on Gradgrind's system of education: he is its star pupil, and has turned out to be a little monster. Bitzer expresses openly the view, implicit in earlier scenes, that modern thought teaches us to look out only for our own interests. He corrects Mrs Sparsit when she says gambling is immoral. Belonging to a younger generation, he is more secular-minded and says that gambling is wrong because it does not pay (p. 127).

labouring children to school three hours of schooling a day were provided for in law, from 1844

quite so much smoke an act of 1847 aimed to control smoke pollution

increased and multiplied an echo of Genesis 9:1

simoom a hot desert wind

the eye of Heaven the sun

Bank Dragon in mythology, dragons commonly guard treasure

a truckle bed on runners, to be put away by day

wafers sticky disks for sealing letters

a Roman matron ... invading general see Shakespeare's *Coriolanus* Act V Scene 3

like the Sultan a legendary Egyptian ruler who saw marvels in a bucket of water

something fluffy bits of raw cotton

CHAPTER 2 MR JAMES HARTHOUSE

James Harthouse, gentleman-cynic, going in for politics, meets Bounderby

Gradgrind heads a group of politicians who support hard-fact economics and the interests of manufacturers. Although they claim to despise aristocrats, they are actually glad to recruit them. James Harthouse, a former cavalry officer and diplomat who is now bored with everything, is the latest of these cynical upper-class recruits. He has come to Coketown to find a parliamentary seat in the district, bringing a recommendation to Bounderby from Gradgrind.

Bounderby is as proud of his low origins, he says, as Harthouse is of his upper-class background: he thinks this makes them equals. He introduces Harthouse to Louisa. Harthouse is intrigued by her pride, sensitivity and repressed emotion. She asks if he hopes to serve his country. He talks with superficial wit, saying he has no beliefs. Most politicians, he claims, only pretend to have beliefs: at least he is honest about being dishonest. Self-interest is the only reality. When Tom arrives late for dinner, Harthouse notices the smile Louisa gives her brother. She cares only for this 'whelp', he decides. He pretends to make friends with Tom and they leave the house together.

> Harthouse depicts a social type, the languid and cynical aristocrat who affects to be bored, that Dickens especially detested. Harthouse is posing. He likes to imply that having seen through everyone else shows he is the cleverest. Dickens's plans for the novel show that he wanted readers to understand that Harthouse's cynical admission of selfishness is morally equivalent to Gradgrind's theory of self-interest as the foundation of economics. It is **ironic** that Gradgrind has recommended the man who will attempt to seduce his daughter.

> Bounderby's conversation with Harthouse illustrates what was said in the previous chapter about the attitude of the Coketown factory-owners. Bounderby offers to summarise the essential points of the Coketown question. 'Our smoke,' he says, is 'the healthiest thing in the world ... and particularly for the lungs' (p. 130). Coketown will not reduce emissions 'for all the humbugging sentiment in Great Britain'. As for the hands, they expect to be fed on turtle soup and venison with gold spoons.

Graces three Greek goddesses representing charm, beauty and grace respectively

railway accident this topic had recently been debated in the House of Lords, in February 1854

a Cornet of dragoons a junior cavalry officer

minister ambassador

muster-roll an army list; Harthouse is Gradgrind's political recruit

hack work-horse

What will be, will be the motto of the Russell family

polonies and saveloys sausages that sometimes contained horsemeat

CHAPTER 3 THE WHELP

Harthouse, 'agreeable demon', drinks with Tom 'the whelp', and learns about Louisa

While they drink and smoke together, Harthouse impresses Tom with his relaxed air and knowledge of the world. Tom quickly gets drunk and brags that Louisa only married Bounderby for his sake. Harthouse despises 'the whelp' but is glad of the information. When Tom leaves Harthouse's hotel, the narrator says the whelp might as well go and drown himself in the canal.

> This scene, where Harthouse seems so sure of himself, kicking Tom awake with his boot, prepares for the later confrontation between Sissy and Harthouse in the same room, in Book III Chapter 2, where she quells him, makes him feel that this time he is 'the whelp', and in effect kicks him out of Coketown for good.

> **Verb neuter** Tom mimics reciting a conjugation at school
> **flat** stupid, naïve
> **set her cap at** aimed to marry

CHAPTER 4 MEN AND BROTHERS

Denounced by the 'froth and fume' orator Slackbridge, Stephen refuses to join the union and is ostracised

Slackbridge the trade union delegate addresses a large audience of working men, calling them 'slaves' and 'brothers'. The narrator contrasts the earnest, thoughtful faces of the workers with the 'froth and fume' and 'fiery face' of their leader (p. 142), and comments that a crowd will submit to crude oratory, and, as in this case, in a mistaken cause. Slackbridge says there is a traitor in their midst. The chairman calls for the accused man, Stephen Blackpool.

Stephen is the only hand who has refused to join the United Aggregate Tribunal. He admits he has no faith in the union, but insists his reasons for staying out are different and personal. Stephen's dignity is impressive; many sympathise. Stephen says he knows he will now be totally ostracised; he does not protest. He only asks to be allowed to work on; he has no other livelihood.

Stephen begins a painfully lonely life, avoided by all, and avoiding Rachael for fear she might be implicated in his disgrace. After four days, Bitzer summons him to Bounderby's house.

Dickens's unsympathetic depiction of the trade union has aroused hostile comment from many critics. Dickens included union leaders in his sweeping, perhaps unreasonable, dislike of politicians. Many readers will think him shortsighted in his rejection of unionism, and regard this scene as a weakness in the novel. Some historians point out that in the case of the strike at Preston, still in progress when the novel began to appear in *Household Words*, the mill-workers underwent prolonged deprivation for no immediate advantage.

Another possible objection to this scene is that Stephen's refusal to join the union is inadequately motivated. Dickens always sympathised with the individual victim of an institution; some might feel that Dickens chose to make Stephen a victim (see Characterisation).

birthright for a mess of pottage Esau sold his birthright to his brother Jacob for bread and soup; see Genesis 25:29–34

Judas Iscariot he betrayed Jesus for thirty pieces of silver; see Matthew 26:14–16

Castlereagh Lord Castlereagh (1769–1822) was remembered for his role in suppressing by military force a meeting in favour of parliamentary reform at St Peter's (Peterloo) Fields, Manchester, 16 August 1819, where many people were injured and eleven killed

ashes asks

hetter eager

awlung because

liefer rather

moydert puzzled

awlus always

Strike o' day daybreak

fratch quarrel

Gonnows God knows

turn out strike
Roman Brutus Lucius Junius Brutus, said to have executed his sons for treason
The Spartan mothers famous for bellicosity
fugleman other soldiers marched in step with him

CHAPTER 5 MEN AND MASTERS

Stephen contradicts Bounderby and loses his job

Bounderby receives Stephen in his drawing room, where Louisa, Tom and Harthouse are present. Hating the union, Bounderby is at first sympathetic, but soon turns less friendly, and is further antagonised when Stephen admits he would have joined the union except for a private promise.

When he senses sympathy in Louisa, Stephen's tongue is loosened and he makes a firm but moderate speech in favour of his fellow-workers. Incensed, Bounderby orders Stephen to explain what the workers complain of. Stephen speaks of the hardships of the labourers' lives, concluding that all is 'a muddle'. Pressed to recommend a solution, he says it is for those 'set above' the workers to find it. Bounderby says they will at least put a stop to Slackbridge. Stephen rashly contradicts him, insisting that 'mischievous strangers', as the employers call them, are not the root of the problem. Bounderby is enraged.

Louisa signals that it would be wise to leave, but Stephen, now strongly moved, delivers a final speech. 'Letting alone' (laissez-faire) is not the answer; nor can the people solve the muddle; above all, treating people like figures in a sum, or like machines, will not serve. Bounderby is now so angry that he dismisses Stephen, with his customary bluntness, from his job.

> This scene is **ironic** in several ways. Although silenced by his fellow-workers, Stephen acts as their spokesmen, perhaps provoked by his four days of silence into saying more than is prudent. When he addresses a speech to Louisa, it seems as though Bounderby has been sent to Coventry. The 'plain man' Bounderby cannot stand plain speaking.

There is mounting drama throughout the scene, with Bounderby's 'windiness' (p. 149) increasing to 'a hurricane' (p. 153), and Stephen gradually led on to express openly his normally guarded views.

'Muddle' may seem an inadequate term. Readers who approve what Stephen says about the condition of the poor may regret his docile appeal to those 'set above us', the so-called 'masters' of the chapter title, to solve the 'muddle'. In his last speech, however, Stephen voices Dickens's own specific rejection of the 'laissez-faire' or 'lettin alone' principle and of statistics and men-as-machines mentality ('reg'latin 'em as if they was figures in a soom [sum], or machines', p. 154). When he hears this, the main thrust of the novel's argument, uttered by a workman, the Coketown master sacks the man.

Although Louisa sympathises with Stephen, she is powerless to help him, or to say anything at all. This is a culture in which men do the talking about serious matters. Ironically, by silently giving him the sense of a sympathiser, Louisa encourages Stephen to speak against his own interests. Her situation parallels Stephen's in some respects. Bounderby will in due course dismiss her too.

transportation sending convicts to colonial labour camps
Chrisen Christian
ahint behind
to card to extract impurities from cotton
Norfolk Island a south-Pacific penal colony

CHAPTER 6 FADING

> **Who is Mrs Pegler? Why does Tom tell Stephen to linger near the bank after work until he leaves? Stephen and Rachael part**

Leaving Bounderby's house, Stephen finds Rachael with the old country-woman he met there once before, now eager to hear about Mrs Bounderby. Stephen and Rachael invite her to tea. The old woman, Mrs Pegler, once had a son but has 'lost' him. Louisa and Tom arrive. Louisa offers Stephen money, but he will only take £2, as a loan. He is moved to tears by her kindness. On the stairs Tom tells Stephen to wait near the bank after work every day until he leaves Coketown; perhaps Tom will send him a message offering help. Tom, Louisa and Mrs Pegler leave. Stephen and Rachael say goodbye. Stephen waits near the bank on each of his remaining three days of piece-work, and then leaves Coketown.

More links are created among the characters. Tom's plot against Stephen begins here, preparing for the closing stages of the story when Stephen is a wanted man. Never afraid to use coincidence, Dickens does so here in twice bringing Mrs Pegler to Coketown for her once-a-year visit on the day Stephen visits Bounderby's house. This is a connection we are invited to wonder about.

The fact that Louisa now enters a workman's house for the first time in her life allows Dickens an **ironic** comment on all the abstract knowledge she has gained about the workforce in her father's system of education.

Stephen speaks too mildly, for some readers, here and in the last chapter. A very different voice can be heard in this chapter, addressing all Gradgrinds or Bounderbys, and warning of revolution. This is one of the places where the narrative voice becomes that of Dickens as author and public man, declaiming in a style reminiscent of Thomas Carlyle (see Literary Background): 'in the day of your triumph, when romance is utterly driven out of their souls [referring to people like Stephen and Rachael], and they and a bare existence stand face to face, Reality will take a wolfish turn, and make an end of you' (p. 166). The rhythm of these lines is close to that of **blank verse**, as sometimes happens in passages where Dickens addresses the reader in this way (see Textual Analysis, Text 2).

leesom cheerful
hey-go-mad excited
Lord Chesterfield (1694–1773) author of *Letters to his Son* (1774), rules for polite conduct, a book valued by many, but not by Dickens
the poor … always with you see Matthew 26:11

CHAPTER 7 GUNPOWDER

Bounderby is now a country gentleman. Harthouse wins Louisa's confidence and her smile. Tom has unpaid gambling debts

Bounderby has acquired a country house near Coketown. He exults over its previous owner, a gentleman called Nickits, now bankrupt, and rejoices in his own continuing rise in the world. James Harthouse is a promising political candidate. He explains to Louisa that, while all politicians are hypocrites, he is one of the few who are honest enough to admit it. Harthouse is playing with Louisa. He will enjoy a new sensation if she smiles for him as she does for the whelp. He likes entering her confidence and showing he knows her true feelings for her husband and her brother. She tells him about Tom's gambling debts, some of which she has settled by selling jewellery. Harthouse talks to Tom and offers help. Tearing up rosebuds as he talks, Tom grumbles that Louisa has not raised more money for him, and says help is now too late. He is briefly in tears. Harthouse persuades him to be nicer to his sister, and is later rewarded by Louisa's smile.

> The narrator stresses that Harthouse's cynicism is no worse than Gradgrind's materialism: both deny all human and spiritual values. (Dickens's working notes stress his aim to show this moral equivalence.) We hear that 'it was as much against the precepts of [Harthouse's] school to wonder, as it was against the doctrines of the Gradgrind College' (p. 179). Harthouse's views are indeed welcome to Louisa because they reassure her that her father was right, and that her long-suppressed hopes and yearnings have been a delusion. The gunpowder trail indicated by the chapter title goes back to the early days of Louisa's 'training'.

> Harthouse is worse than a normal seducer because, lacking vitality, he plays with Louisa and experiments on her, as her father did with his system. He is called a 'powerful Familiar' (p. 177) or devil; the philosophy, by implication, is also diabolical.

> **Ironically,** Harthouse offers to help Tom with money just too late to save him from robbing the bank. The red roses

are contrasted to Tom's whiteness when he hears about 'bankers', one of many passages of colour imagery. Tom's tearing of the rosebuds **symbolises** the waste of his life and of Louisa's, perhaps Harthouse's as well since he throws away some roses too (p. 179).

'Nickits' is oddly close to being an anagram of 'Dickens'.

'going in' ... to score as in cricket

Gorgon (Greek mythology) a female monster

depth answers unto depth Psalms 42:7

blacking bottles a covert allusion to Dickens's childhood (see Charles Dickens's Life and Work)

Westminster School a famous boys' school in London, known for its long tradition of an annual Latin play

Antwerp English bankrupts often settled there

Arcadian ideal, as though in the golden age pictured in classical Greek poetry

Familiar evil spirit

CHAPTER 8 EXPLOSION

Robbery at the bank. Stephen and Mrs Pegler suspected. Louisa suspects Tom

Early next morning Harthouse congratulates himself on his power over Louisa's feelings. As he rides out for his day's political activities, Bounderby accosts him with stunning news: the bank has been robbed of £150. Louisa, Mrs Sparsit and Bitzer join them. Bounderby suspects Stephen Blackpool, because he has been seen loitering near the bank, and an old woman has also been seen hanging about, and going to Stephen's lodgings. They must have belonged to a gang. Mrs Sparsit's nerves have been so upset that she is obliged to leave the bank and stay at Bounderby's for some time. Louisa has also had a shock, because she suspects Tom. Going to his room at night she lies beside him, cradling him like a child and begs him to confess. He does not, but weeps when she has gone. Mrs Sparsit calls Louisa 'Miss Gradgrind', and tries to take over the household.

The bank robbery is an effective plot device, which eventually involves most of the characters in its consequences. As we see here, many are already affected: Bounderby, Harthouse, Mrs Sparsit, Bitzer, Louisa, Stephen, Mrs Pegler and Tom. His guilt will later involve Gradgrind, Sissy and Mr Sleary. Tom's having put the blame on Stephen connects the two main strands of the book, which we can now identify: one involving Gradgrind's family, and the theme of education, the other Stephen and Bounderby and the theme of industrial labour (see Structure).

The sum of £150 would not have been a very serious loss to a Victorian banker. Bounderby is more upset by the affront of a robbery than by the sum involved. For ordinary people, however, it was a large amount; and such a robbery would have been regarded as a serious crime, to be punished accordingly. Tom is terrified from now on.

The lines about Tom's despair, 'rejecting all the good in the world', imply that his soul is in danger. Harthouse's sport with Louisa is plainly said to be devilish, in the passage about devilry on page 181. He has also been amusing himself, rather than seriously trying to be of help, in his relations with Tom.

Some critics find Louisa's cuddling of Tom incestuous. Whatever we think of that, we can observe in this section of the chapter that Louisa and Bounderby have separate bedrooms.

Mrs Sparsit's unwillingness to say 'Mrs Bounderby' may recall Mrs Gradgrind's inability to say 'Josiah' (p. 105). Harthouse's misnaming of Stephen as 'Blackpot' (p. 185) is a mark of his indifference.

Bounderby uses a fanciful, fairy-story image when he playfully pictures the old woman we know as Mrs Pegler flying into Coketown on a broomstick, like a witch (p. 187). This is a jest which, we are already likely to guess, will rebound upon him. It is a clever **ironic** touch made possible by the careful plotting. There is another ironic touch in the fact that the 'gang' that met in Stephen's lodgings included Louisa and Tom, as well as Mrs Pegler.

Dickens brings in Bitzer here, and in the next chapter, in order to keep him in our minds. The story keeps all the characters in play.

legion see Mark 5:9, where devils possessing a man give themselves this name

a roaring lion 1 Peter 5:8

brimstone Revelation 21:8

as if it were a tambourine like an oriental dancer in the London streets

'Alas poor Yorick!' see *Hamlet* Act V Scene 1 line 202

CHAPTER 9 HEARING THE LAST OF IT

Mrs Sparsit spies on Harthouse and Louisa. Mrs Gradgrind dies, trying to leave a message about life

Mrs Sparsit darts about, nimbly spying on Louisa and Harthouse. Behind his back she likes saying 'Noodle!' to Bounderby's portrait.

Bitzer arrives with a note. Louisa is to visit her mother, who is gravely ill. She rarely goes to Stone Lodge now. Her father is often away 'at his parliamentary cinder-heap in London' (p. 198), and Louisa lacks the tender memories that ought to tie her to her childhood home. Mrs Gradgrind is dying, as vaguely as she has lived. She hardly knows if her pain is her own. When Louisa's younger sister Jane comes in with Sissy, it seems Sissy's influence has been a happier one than Louisa ever knew. Mrs Gradgrind wants to send a message to her husband to say there is something, not in any 'Ology' [science], that he and she have forgotten. She has no pen but tries to write the missing word 'of wonderful no-meaning' (p. 201) with her hand on the bedclothes as she dies.

Mrs Sparsit's successful efforts to take over the role of housekeeper result in Louisa's depending more on Harthouse for company.

This chapter illustrates the odd relations between comic and serious effects in *Hard Times*. It begins with an entertaining picture of Mrs Sparsit as a witch. Although always seen to walk at a ladylike pace, she can move about the house amazingly fast. Does she slide down the banisters? Or can she move in ways unseen by human eyes? It ends with a very different treatment of the unseen. Mrs Gradgrind has always been nearly invisible, a mere 'bundle of shawls' (p. 22);

now she disappears altogether. Her invisible writing of 'wonderful no-meaning' produces a truly uncanny effect, and the closing lines, where she assumes in death 'the dread solemnity of the sages and patriarchs' (p. 201), are impressive, in the Victorian deathbed manner.

This short, memorable scene where Mrs Gradgrind does indeed 'hear the last of it' has attracted much critical comment. (For Jean Ferguson Carr's comments on Mrs Gradgrind as a mother denied her maternal role, in her essay on feminist discourses in *Hard Times*, see Critical History, on Feminist Criticism).

The 'wonderful no-meaning', an **ironic** reference to Gradgrind's abolition of everything but fact, prepares for his eventual recognition of the power of a loving heart. 'Heart', represented in this scene by Sissy's presence, is stressed in many passages in the following chapters.

express urgent letter

suffering little children see Mark 10:14–15

grapes are ... thistles see Matthew 7:16

nearer Truth according to the Greek philosopher Democritus, truth lies at the bottom of a well; that is, somewhere hard to find

disquieteth himself in vain echoes the Order for the Burial of the Dead in the Book of Common Prayer: 'for man walketh in a vain shadow, and disquieteth himself in vain'

CHAPTER 10 MRS SPARSIT'S STAIRCASE

Mrs Sparsit enjoys daydreaming of Louisa's adultery and disgrace. Harthouse preaches cynicism

Mrs Sparsit's nerves are slow to mend. She continues to fawn on Bounderby and say 'Noodle' to his portrait. Even when she does go back to the bank, she returns for weekends. She has started to enjoy picturing Louisa walking down a great staircase towards a pit of shame and ruin. Louisa chats with Harthouse. She cannot believe Stephen guilty; he takes it for granted in his cynical way. Morality is only talk, he says. Mrs Sparsit spies on them from a distance. Bounderby plans to wait for the thieves to betray themselves.

Mrs Sparsit has invented the image of the staircase, although she is 'not a poetical woman' (p. 202), we are told by the very poetical narrator. While reiteration of the image shows us Mrs Sparsit's growing obsession with the prospect of Louisa's downfall, Dickens also takes advantage of it to increase suspense, using 'Lower and Lower' for the next chapter title, for example, and 'Down' for the one after that.

Romulus and Remus the legendary founders of Rome, abandoned in infancy and suckled by a she-wolf

under the rose in secret

Giant's Staircase in the Ducal Palace in Venice

CHAPTER 11 LOWER AND LOWER

Mrs Sparsit in hiding hears Harthouse tell Louisa he loves her. She follows Louisa but loses her

Mr Gradgrind buries his wife and returns to his duties in Parliament, 'the national cinder-heap' (p. 206). Mrs Sparsit visits Bounderby's country house one weekend when he is away after learning that Harthouse has tricked Tom into staying away too. She has rightly guessed that Harthouse has planned to be alone with Louisa. This time she spies on them from a hiding place close enough to overhear Harthouse declare his love. She rejoices when Harthouse puts an arm around Louisa. She follows when Louisa leaves the house, but loses track of her in torrential rain at the railway station in Coketown.

Dickens continues to have fun with fanciful **images** of Mrs Sparsit. She has been a witch, Coriolanus's mother, a Dragon, and in this chapter she becomes Robinson Crusoe, hiding in the woods (p. 211).

As the tension mounts, the characters begin to speak **melodramatically**. 'Harthouse is with his [Tom's] sister now!' hisses Mrs Sparsit to herself (p. 209), and Harthouse speaks of 'cruel commands' and being 'prostrate' under Louisa's foot (p. 212). The weather is also melodramatic, as on the night of Stephen's dream, but the pouring rain will in due course help the comic treatment of Mrs Sparsit, drenching and bedraggling her out of all her grand-lady pretensions, and punishing her with a bad cold.

India ale bottled for export
Furies (Greek mythology) fearsome goddesses who punish and avenge
caught up in a cloud like the prophet Elijah; see 2 Kings 2:11
electric wires telegraph wires ran beside the railways from the late 1840s
Robinson Crusoe ... savages in Defoe's novel, Crusoe and Friday attack cannibals from the shelter of a wood

CHAPTER 12 DOWN

A storm breaks. Louisa flees to her father and tells him everything

Mr Gradgrind is at home in his study when Louisa arrives in a thunderstorm, soaked and distressed. She delivers a passionate speech, melodramatic in style, cursing the hour in which she was born, wishing he had taught her to obey her heart, admitting that she has come close, though not yet 'disgraced', to yielding to Harthouse, and imploring him to save her by some new lesson of the heart, since all the old teaching has proved useless. Finally Louisa, 'the pride of his heart and the triumph of his system', falls at his feet (p. 219). Gradgrind is deeply moved.

> The point of the chapter title, which threatened 'ruin' in the sense Mrs Sparsit is hoping for, is revealed in the last words, where Louisa falls at her father's feet, and not into the pit of shame.
>
> Louisa's long sentences and melodramatic exclamations are far removed from what such a young woman might actually have said in the circumstances. Louisa has presumably never even entered a Victorian theatre. Later in the nineteenth century such effects came to seem dated and perhaps ridiculous. Readers today are better placed to appreciate that Dickens and many of his readers found melodrama the appropriate mode for such a dramatic and emotional scene, and to accept Louisa's speeches as the novelist's version of what she so desperately wants to say (see Characterisation, and Language & Style).

This scene parallels, but perhaps does not equal in artistry, the previous scene between Louisa and her father, in the same room, in Book I Chapter 15 (see Textual Analysis, Text 2).

the national dustmen Members of Parliament
the Good Samaritan see Luke 10:29–37 where the good Samaritan gives money and help to a stranger in distress

BOOK THE THIRD: GARNERING

CHAPTER 1 ANOTHER THING NEEDFUL

Gradgrind begins to learn about the reasons of the heart. Louisa welcomes Sissy's healing love

Louisa wakes in her old bed at home. She comments on her sister Jane's un-Gradgrindlike beaming face. Jane says that must be Sissy's doing, but Louisa is still unwilling to hear about Sissy. Mr Gradgrind is trying to adjust to what he heard from Louisa last night. Humbly, he admits responsibility for the failure of his 'system'. He confesses he hardly knows now how to help; having always relied on the wisdom of the head, he must perhaps begin to learn that of the heart. He wonders if 'mere love and gratitude' may in his absence in London have brought about the change to be seen in Jane (p. 226). These last words refer to the influence of Sissy. When Gradgrind has gone out, Sissy enters the bedroom and lays her hand on Louisa's neck. 'Let it lie there …' the narrator exclaims (p. 227). Louisa confesses her pride, hardness and lack of the simplest true education. She lays her head on Sissy's loving heart.

> Gradgrind's gentle caressing of Louisa's hair, a show of tenderness so unusual that she 'takes it for a speech of contrition', is effective use of gesture. Gradgrind has had far too much to say in the past. It is one of many moments in the novel when silence or silent communication is emphasised. These often involve female characters. Gradgrind's being here at a loss for words is the beginning of his reformation and of the change in the reader's intended sympathies (see Critical History, on Feminist Criticism).

Louisa has been estranged from Sissy ever since she noticed the other girl's look of pity on hearing of her marriage. Now, with the ending of her marriage, she is reunited with Sissy.

There is another use of the phrase 'let it' in the exclamation 'let it lie there', echoing Louisa's words when she consents to marry Bounderby: 'Let it be so' (p. 103).

Another Thing Needful see the title of Book I Chapter 1
excise rod a measuring stick for assessing duty

CHAPTER 2 VERY RIDICULOUS

Sissy tells Harthouse that he will never see Louisa again. He submits

James Harthouse is agitated, for once, when he receives no word from Louisa. Perhaps her irate husband will come instead. Actually, it is Sissy who confronts him in his hotel room, informs him where Louisa is, tells him he is never to see her again, and orders him to leave Coketown for good. It may be very ridiculous of him to submit, but he does so, conscious of his weak position, but even more aware of Sissy's innocence, integrity and firmness. He asks who she is, and learns she is a stroller's child. Harthouse decides to go on his travels, again, this time up the Nile.

This powerful scene is usually regarded as a striking success, although some critics have called it unrealistic. George Bernard Shaw objected that the 'dunce' of the local school would not be able to speak, as Sissy does, with the fluent authority of a Lord Chief Justice. Dickens wanted to persuade us that she deserves to be a judge because her heart is pure; his low opinion of actual judges can be seen in *Bleak House*. The brief duel between Sissy and Harthouse is one of heart rather than head, and Harthouse is 'touched in the cavity where his heart should have been' (p. 234) (see Characterisation).

This scene parallels the one in Book II Chapter 3, where Harthouse and Tom talk in the same hotel room. On that occasion Harthouse has the upper hand. Now he feels he is 'the whelp'.

glass in its eye monocle

griffin a mythical animal, with an eagle's head and wings on a lion's body

wrestle ... in the Lancashire manner Lancashire wrestling was especially dangerous

the Holy Office ... tortures the Roman Catholic Inquisition, notorious for torture in earlier times

the swell mob smartly dressed pickpockets

CHAPTER 3 VERY DECIDED

Bounderby returns to Coketown and refuses to sympathise. He and Louisa will live apart

Still bedraggled from the storm and suffering from a bad cold, Mrs Sparsit rushes to London to tell Bounderby the shocking news, and he rushes her back to Coketown where he finds Louisa at Stone Lodge. Gradgrind tries to explain his own altered views on life, and pleads for Louisa to stay on at Stone Lodge for a while. Bounderby insists on a separation, unless she will return at once. Mrs Sparsit is sent back to the bank.

This chapter emphasises the contrast between Gradgrind and Bounderby that has been implicit throughout the story. They are different types of character. Bounderby predictably declares that imagination means 'turtle soup, venison and a golden spoon'. He cannot change his outlook or his lines. Although he is now developing new sympathies, Gradgrind remains his old rational self when, naïvely, he expects Bounderby to be reasonable. This intellectual consistency helps make his change of heart more convincing (see Textual Analysis, Text 3).

St James's Street an expensive part of fashionable London

Cock-and-a-Bull tall story

lights opinions

Rocket probably a sky-rocket; but possibly George Stephenson's famous locomotive

candle-snuff burnt wick of a candle

chapter 4 lost

Bounderby makes Stephen a wanted man. His friends want him to return, but he cannot be found

Bounderby renews his interest in the investigation of the bank robbery. He puts up posters offering a £20 reward for the arrest of Stephen Blackpool, and Slackbridge publicises it further at a union meeting.

Bounderby, Tom and Rachael call on Gradgrind, wanting to see Louisa. Rachael reports what happened on the day Louisa lent Stephen £2, and Louisa confirms the truth of her account, to Bounderby's surprise. Tom is very uneasy. Rachael says she has written to Stephen today. He is sure to return to clear his name. Louisa pities Stephen; Bounderby does not. Later, Rachael and Louisa discuss Stephen's plight.

Gradgrind is impressed by the women's confidence in Stephen's innocence. But who else could the thief be? He is looking old and tired. Louisa and Sissy agree to protect him by not talking in his presence about this dangerous subject.

Rachael expected Stephen to return within two days. On the fourth day, Rachel produces his address and messengers are sent, but Stephen has disappeared. When there is still no sign of him after a week, Tom looks much happier.

> Where is Stephen, and what will happen to Tom? Suspense over these two questions, raised in this chapter, will mount from now on until the story ends. It is of interest that the women, Rachael, Sissy and Louisa, take active roles at this stage, while Tom and Gradgrind are helpless. Bounderby, too, is at a loss, and a serious reversal awaits him in the next chapter.
>
> Tom keeps close to Bounderby during the discussion of Stephen's guilt, and they leave together. It is Bounderby, not his father, whom he relies on now.
>
> The look exchanged between Louisa and Sissy (p. 255) signifies, as we learn later, that they have both worked out that Tom must be guilty. This is another of the silent but meaningful exchanges between women which make a contrast to the long,

often absurd speeches made by men (see Themes, on Lives of Women).

Venus (Roman mythology) the goddess of love who sprang to life from the foam of the sea
sheet-anchor the most reliable support
like the serpent in the garden see Genesis 3:4

CHAPTER 5 FOUND

Rachael and Sissy still believe in Stephen. Mrs Sparsit catches Bounderby's mother

More days pass but Stephen remains missing. Sissy comforts Rachael. Fearing Stephen may have been murdered, Rachael is becoming ill. Sissy offers to go for a country walk with her on Sunday.

As they are passing Bounderby's house, they see Mrs Sparsit pulling Mrs Pegler along. Bounderby is furious, because this is his mother. Far from having abandoned him as a baby, it turns out that she gave him a good start in life. Although theirs was a poor family, Bounderby's tales of early sufferings are lies. He has paid his mother to keep out of the way. All Coketown will soon be talking about the 'self-made Humbug' (p. 264). Mrs Sparsit is also in disgrace. Gradgrind remarks to Sissy and Louisa that Mrs Pegler's innocence of the robbery lifts suspicion from Stephen. There is still no sign of the missing man.

> The chapter title is deliberately misleading: we expect Stephen to be found, not Bounderby's mother. Mrs Pegler's capture by Mrs Sparsit and Bounderby's discomfiture provide comic relief. The gathering of a crowd inside Bounderby's dining room is an example of Dickens's willingness to sacrifice probability to drama. It is dramatically effective and appropriate that his lies should be exposed before a large audience.

> At the end of the chapter the mood changes, with references to the 'awful fear' (of Tom's guilt) which 'hovers … like a ghostly shadow' over Louisa and Sissy (p. 265). Gradgrind has been badly shocked by Louisa's breakdown, with its implied discrediting – for he is a

logical man – of his hard-fact system of education. Now it seems likely that Tom's 'model' education will prove to have had even worse results.

cypher to do arithmetic
Slough of Despond in *Pilgrim's Progress* the hero Christian falls into this allegorical swamp of dejection, but is rescued by Help

CHAPTER 6 THE STARLIGHT

> **Stephen is found, deep in an uncovered pit-shaft. He prays for better understanding, asks Gradgrind to clear his name, and dies confident in his religious faith**

On Sunday, Sissy and Louisa walk in the countryside and find a hat lying in the grass. Nearby is the edge of an uncovered pit-shaft. Rachael bursts into hysterical tears when they see Stephen's name in the hat. The women find help; a message is sent to Stone Lodge. The construction of a windlass takes all day. Gradgrind, Louisa and Tom arrive. Finally Stephen is found alive but mortally hurt. It is learnt that he fell while hurrying to Bounderby's house to plead his innocence.

Night falls and torches are lit. At last Stephen's broken body is raised to the surface, arousing a murmur of pity from the crowd. Stephen talks about the shaft where he has lain for over a week, with some water and a little food. Many others have died here because the mine-owners will not pay to cover such shafts. All is a muddle. He gazes up at a star which was shining into the shaft and gave him comfort. Gradgrind promises to clear Stephen's name. Ask your son how, Stephen says. They carry him through the fields on a stretcher, Rachael holding his hand. 'It was soon a funeral procession.'

> Dickens arouses emotion in this scene. He insists on Stephen's Christian death: 'The star had shown him where to find the God of the poor; and through humility, and sorrow, and forgiveness, he had gone to his Redeemer's rest' (p. 275). Lying in the shaft, he assumed Louisa was part of Tom's plot to incriminate him, but the starlight taught him to forgive her. His dying prayer is that 'aw' th' world may on'y coom toogether more' – that all the world may only come together more (p. 273). The emotion generated by a

sympathetic character's death is used to endorse the novel's appeal for social harmony.

The chapter also stresses the goodwill of the working people who volunteer to spend Sunday, their only rest-day, toiling to rescue Stephen. Dickens's hostility to the Sabbatarian movement, which aimed to restrict Sunday recreations, and to the Teetotal Society, is also apparent, in the **ironic** comment on the larks singing 'although it was Sunday' (p. 265), and in repeated references to the workman who is drunk when Sissy appeals for help, but quickly sobers up and becomes the leader of the rescue party. In contrast to these impressions of the goodwill of ordinary people, there are renewed attacks, in what Stephen says, on the indifference of factory and mine-owners to the safety of their employees. He refers again to Rachael's little sister, who died 'young and misshapen', because of 'sickly air' (p. 273).

There are readers who find Stephen's death (like many such scenes in Dickens) unduly sentimental, and his lengthy dying-speeches unrealistic. Perhaps some of the sentimental touches are better than others. Readers who wish Dickens had used the **symbol** of the star with more restraint can also be moved when Stephen (referring back to her earlier warnings that they should not be seen too often together) tells Rachael that they may walk together tonight, and she promises to keep beside him 'all the way' (p. 274).

Rachael's hysterical outburst on realising that Stephen has fallen into the shaft shows how strong her love for him has always been, although restrained by Victorian propriety.

sackcloth a sign of penance; this passage alludes to Sabbatarianism

a hurdle a piece of fencing

Fire-damp an explosive gas

CHAPTER 7 WHELP-HUNTING

> Tom is at Sleary's circus. His father's plans to help him
> escape are thwarted by Bitzer

Sissy whispered something in Tom's ear at the Old Hell Shaft, causing him to slip away from the scene. His absence finally convinces his father that he is guilty. Gradgrind is now looking old and defeated, yet more dignified than when he used to pose as the champion of hard-fact philosophy. He tells Louisa and Sissy that he wants to help Tom escape abroad before making public Stephen's innocence. Sissy says she has sent Tom to take refuge with Mr Sleary, now at a nearby town. It is within a train-journey of the port of Liverpool, where Tom can be smuggled abroad.

Louisa and Sissy arrive at the circus, followed by Gradgrind. Tom, disguised in comic costume, confesses to the robbery, adding that it is a statistical fact that a certain proportion of employees will prove dishonest. He is put into a new disguise for his journey to the train. Gradgrind gives him his blessing and a letter for his agent at Liverpool. Tom manages a few sobs, but rebukes Louisa for letting him down, reducing her to genuine tears.

Bitzer now makes a dramatic appearance, having spied on Gradgrind. He collars Tom.

> Circus life is vividly conveyed, and once more contrasted to Gradgrindery. Sleary welcomes Sissy and Louisa and talks about the company. He is willing to help 'the Thquire' for Sissy's sake. Sissy meets her old friends. Master Kidderminster now has a beard. There is a new clown. It is **symbolically** appropriate for Gradgrind, formerly the enemy of all the circus stands for, to hear his son's confession in the circus ring, with the acrobats and comedians of Sleary's company in the background. Seated on a clown's chair, he contemplates his 'model-son' in the costume and face-blacking for a comic turn.

> It is also **ironic** that Tom defends himself by referring to statistics, which Gradgrind would formerly have said were the only facts of the matter. In becoming a thief, Tom has put into practice another of Gradgrind's economic doctrines, that self-interest is fundamental. Tom's total lack of feeling for his sister emphasises the point that all natural feeling has been destroyed by his upbringing. This child of Fact presents a complete contrast to the circus child Sissy. Another product of the school of Fact appears at the end of this chapter in the person of Bitzer, who has been linked with and contrasted to Sissy since the first scene of the novel.

play a Roman part to sacrifice a relation to justice
Grand Morning Performance theatre language for an afternoon performance
Athley'th Astley's Theatre in London (see Historical Background, on
Circuses)
beadle constable
Jothkin Joskin, country bumpkin

CHAPTER 8 PHILOSOPHICAL

**Utilitarian Bitzer knows no mercy. Sleary helps Tom
escape, and reaffirms circus philosophy**

Bitzer means to denounce Tom and take his job at the bank as his reward.
Gradgrind pleads in vain. Has Bitzer no heart? Yes, but only a physical
one. Self-interest dictates his conduct. Has he no gratitude for his
training in the model-school? No, the fees were paid. Bitzer has,
ironically, all his old lessons pat. But the rational Bitzer is no match for
Sleary, who sends him off, with Tom as his prisoner, behind a horse that
will not stop dancing, and a sagacious dog which pins Bitzer down while
Tom escapes. Gradgrind rewards the company. Sleary recounts the tale
of Merrylegs, Sissy's father's performing dog, which mysteriously found
its way home to the circus to die. The dog would never have left its
master alive, so Sissy's father must now be dead. They will never know
why he deserted her. Gradgrind says that she still keeps her father's old
bottle of 'nine oils' for tending bruises. There is a love in the world, says
Sleary, which has nothing to do with self-interest. It calculates in ways as
mysterious as the uncanny powers of dogs like Merrylegs.

Finally, draining another of his many brandy-and-waters, Sleary
restates his philosophy of life: 'People mutht be amuthed ...' (p. 292). He
never thought, he adds, that he could be such a Cackler.

> Gradgrind's disillusionment with the rule of nothing-but-fact, and
> the novel's demonstration of its falseness, is complete when Bitzer
> repeats his old lessons back to his teacher. To rub the irony in,
> Bitzer is made to speak like a textbook: '... the whole social system
> is a question of self-interest ... We are so constituted' (p. 287).
> Then he calls this lesson the 'catechism' he was taught when very
> young, in Gradgrind's school. 'Catechism' is another of the novel's
> many ironic uses of religious language.

Bitzer's unhappy experience with the dancing horse is an amusing and ironic reminder of his confidence about what a horse is, in Book I Chapter 2.

'Cackler' is a word we have heard before, when Sissy's father was said to have 'his points as a Cackler', although nobody could 'get a living out of *them*' (p. 38). Cackling, the circus term for a clown's patter or banter in the ring, may have amused Dickens as a point of contact between circus arts and his own. Sleary speaks at the end for every artist and entertainer.

The bottle of 'nine oils' kept by Sissy in the hope of her father's return is a small, effective **symbol** of her soothing love.

Harvey William Harvey (1578–1657), English physician, who first demonstrated the circulation of the blood

drag a privately owned coach

Luth lush, alcoholic drinks

CHAPTER 9 FINAL

Bounderby dismisses Mrs Sparsit. The characters' future lives are foreseen. All things move to their appointed ends

Bounderby dismisses Mrs Sparsit. She faces a dismal future as companion to her selfish bed-ridden relative Lady Scadgers, but she has at least the satisfaction of saying 'Noodle' to Bounderby's face.

How much, the narrator wonders, could Bounderby see of the future? Could he see Bitzer taking Tom's place at the bank? He would not foresee his own death, five years hence, or his efforts to perpetuate his name thwarted by lawyers. His portrait would see all this.

Could Gradgrind foresee his old age passed in the service of Faith, Hope and Charity instead of **utilitarian** theories? What would Louisa see in the fire? Certainly the posters proclaiming Stephen's innocence. Would she foresee Rachael's lifetime of labour? Did she foresee Tom's death abroad, penitent at last? Did she see herself caring for Sissy's happy children? 'These things were to be.'

'Dear reader!' the novel ends, and asks us to care for such things. 'Let them be!'

The questions leave the characters wondering about their futures, but the storyteller's assurances admit of no doubts. All will end as it should. Let us learn to care for what is right. The confident **closure** of this ending may be contrasted with Dickens's difficulty in ending his later novel *Great Expectations*.

The phrase 'Let be', which has occurred at several turning points, is used again in the very last words, as is the image of fire: 'Let them be! We shall sit with lighter bosoms on the hearth, to see the ashes of our fires turn grey and cold.' The titles of the three books point to spring, summer and autumn. The last paragraph, addressed directly from author to reader, might seem to acknowledge the unknown, open future of England in 1854, with winter ahead.

Some readers may want to say it is Dickens who takes leave of us, others, Dickens's narrator. We might say it is one of various Dickensian voices to be heard in the narrative, and especially authorial (see Narrative Techniques, on Point of View).

Our last view of Rachael is artfully done. She first appears as one working woman in the crowd of weavers coming from the factory, but the one Stephen is looking for. The picture of her here, always cheerful, always clad in black, sometimes aiding one broken-down old beggar-woman, allows her to fade back into the anonymity of the crowd of unknown women she represents.

Faith, Hope, and Charity see 1 Corinthians 13:1–3
Writing on the Wall a forecast of doom; see Daniel 5

PART THREE

CRITICAL APPROACHES

CHARACTERISATION

A practical way to think about a character in Dickens is to consider how an actor might interpret the role in a stage or screen adaptation. There are some characters who always use pet phrases such as Bounderby's 'turtle soup, venison and a gold spoon', and characteristic gestures such as Mrs Sparsit's raising of her haughty nose or pointing with her mitten. Other roles are more challenging because the character changes in the course of the story. Gradgrind is a tyrant in Book I, but an actor would have to win the audience's sympathy in later scenes.

Characters can also be thought of in terms of the visual arts. Dickens uses pictorial **imagery** for Mrs Sparsit's face: 'her Roman features like a medal struck to commemorate her scorn for Mr Bounderby' (p. 295). The description of Gradgrind in the opening chapter, with its strong and repeated emphasis on a few features, is reminiscent of caricature. Louisa pictured before the fire, watching the sparks fly and wondering about her future, resembles a Victorian 'narrative' painting, where the picture indicates a type of story that viewers are to imagine for themselves.

Characters comment on one another, and sometimes reveal themselves as they do so, as when Bounderby fails to sympathise with Stephen, or when Harthouse calls him 'dreary'. Unexpected encounters like Sissy's with Harthouse also bring out contrasts, showing here the force of her simplicity and the weakness of his sophistication.

Naming is another way of influencing our sense of what a character is like. 'Gradgrind' suggests grinding; when he is reformed, in the last chapter, he is said no longer to grind Faith, Hope and Charity 'in his dusty little mills' (p. 296). Perhaps 'grad' is meant to suggest 'grade', to reflect how obsessed he is with measuring. 'M'Choakumchild' belongs to a long literary tradition of silly **satirical** names; it belongs to the pantomime spirit that runs through the novel. Sleary's name suggests the slur in his speech and the leer in his one fixed eye and one loose one.

Styles of address are also revealing. In the opening scene, Gradgrind calls Sissy 'Girl number twenty' and tells her that 'Sissy' is 'not a name' (p. 11). She must tell her father to call her Cecilia. This is an effective way of conveying his insensitivity. He is deaf to the sound of love in a familiar name. When he says 'Sissy' himself (p. 243), it is a sign he has changed for the better. Mrs Gradgrind says she cannot name Bounderby any more after he becomes engaged to Louisa, because she cannot bear to say 'Josiah' (p. 105). Mrs Sparsit calls Louisa 'Miss Gradgrind' even after her marriage, which she cannot bear to acknowledge. Harthouse's 'Blackpot' for 'Blackpool' shows his indifference to Stephen's fate (p. 185). Such difficulties with names reflect how characters fail to relate.

Dickens wrote to be read aloud, and most of his characters are fluent talkers. Reading aloud, alone or in groups, is a good way to enjoy the characters as talkers. Try Sleary's lisp.

The following notes deal with major characters. There are more comments in Parts Two and Four of the Note.

JOSIAH BOUNDERBY

Bounderby is the villain of the story, heartlessly cruel to Stephen Blackpool, and to Louisa whom he marries without love and repudiates without pity. He represents a social type: the aggressive manufacturer who treats his workers as enemies, bragging of his own achievements as a way of belittling them.

The wrongness of his relation to his workers is shown by the way he has become the victim of his own lies about his early destitution. He has almost come to believe the lies himself. He is punished when his mother tells the true story of his background and reveals him to be a 'self-made Humbug' (p. 264), but he cannot change his nature. Coarse, unfeeling and uncouth, he embodies all Dickens hated in the 'masters' who boasted of their own hardness.

His one merit is his vitality, which makes the role attractive for an actor, or for reading aloud (a different way of speaking the lines). There is gusto as well as absurdity in his recurring sayings. 'I am Josiah Bounderby of Coketown' conveys his pride and enjoyment in the role of plain but powerful man. Others had better not forget to say 'Mr Bounderby, sir'. 'Of Coketown' implies he thinks he owns the place.

Grotesqueness keeps him from becoming a pure figure of fun. When he hugs himself with delight at the thought of Mrs Sparsit's grand connections ('he literally embraced his legs in his great satisfaction and laughed aloud', p. 52), the point is that he is embracing his own body; he is never going to fulfil her hopes and embrace hers. He never ceases to enjoy his pet phrase about the workers' desire for turtle soup, but it comes to seem part of the 'melancholy madness' he shares with his steam engines.

The narrative mocks him with epithets: 'Bully of humility' (p. 21 and often again), or 'blustrous Bounderby' (p. 52). Some images make fun of his pretensions: he is 'a Conqueror' with Mrs Sparsit as 'a captive Princess' (p. 48). Others stress his menace: 'There was a moral infection of clap-trap in him' (p. 49). A 'bounder' later came to mean a cad, perhaps influenced by Dickens's use of 'Bounderby' for a character who overleaps all decent bounds of behaviour.

MRS SPARSIT

Like Bounderby, the housekeeper is absurd and threatening. Even the aristocratic name she is so proud of sounds sinister when she refers to her late husband as 'a Powler' on first meeting Harthouse:

> 'It was once my good or ill fortune, as it may be – before I became a widow – to move in a very different sphere. My husband was a Powler.'
> 'Beg your pardon, really!' said the stranger. 'Was –?' (pp. 124–5).

Mrs Sparsit's nimble movements about Bounderby's house, when pursuing evidence of Louisa's guilt, are also funny and menacing:

> A lady so decorous in herself, and so highly connected, was not to be suspected of dropping over the banisters or sliding down them, yet her extraordinary facility of locomotion suggested the wild idea (p. 194).

Here she plays a part in the novel's pantomime **imagery**, as a comic witch. Another wild idea makes her resemble Shakespeare's Coriolanus, because she has a Roman nose and is haughty. Dickens ridicules the very idea of 'high connections', in Mrs Sparsit, as he ridicules the idea of a 'self-made man' in Bounderby. They are funny and horrible in the way they complement and feed on each other's social fantasies.

Another side to her snobbery is seen in her association with Bitzer. He and she agree in their fear of and contempt for working people, in Book II Chapter 1, a scene where she is far from being just the figure of fun who captures Mrs Pegler and denounces Bounderby as a 'Noodle'. She is more sinister than funny, too, in her voyeur-like spying on Louisa and Harthouse, and her obsessive brooding on Louisa's descent down a great social stairway.

THOMAS GRADGRIND

Gradgrind belongs to a type sometimes termed 'stupid intellectual'. He is an eager but narrow-minded thinker. Intelligent appreciation of advances made in science and social science have mesmerised him into total disregard for the rest of life. Delight in **utilitarian** principles, which aimed to sweep away the past, has unbalanced him and made him fanatical about a brave new world where he thinks nothing will matter but facts and figures. Louisa and Tom are victims of his 'system', and the story teaches him through their downfalls to see where he was wrong. He is able to learn because he is an earnest, well-meaning man, although carried away by ideas.

It is his ability to doubt himself and to change that makes him a different sort of character from Bounderby. That is not obvious when he first appears. In the opening chapters, his repetitions ('fact, fact, fact') and gestures (stabbing the words in with his square head and square forefinger) fix him in our minds as clearly and simply as Bounderby's do. But we gradually find out that he cares about protecting his children from what he truly believes to be the poisonous influence of circuses or fairy stories. His willingness to take in Sissy Jupe also shows his concern with other people. Sleary thinks him worth talking to, in Book I Chapter 5, a scene which also brings out how Bounderby cares about nobody but himself.

Gradgrind's unbalanced state of mind prepares for his breakdown at the end of Book II, and subsequent change of heart, so that he is more credible than some of Dickens's other reformed characters, such as Micawber, for example, whose reformation at the end of *David Copperfield* has struck generations of critics as contrived.

There is a revealing passage soon after Louisa's flight from Bounderby's house, where this voluble, dictatorial speaker communicates with his daughter without words:

> he softly moved her scattered hair from her forehead with his hand. Such little
> actions, slight in another man, were very noticeable in him; and his daughter
> received them as if they had been words of contrition (p. 225).

The defeated and humbled figure of the last chapters remains a man of principle. There is no question, for example, about his resolve to clear Stephen's name. He is consistent in his integrity, although he grows less confident and at the same time more wise. In this respect, he is contrasted with other politicians (p. 276).

LOUISA BOUNDERBY (BORN GRADGRIND)

Louisa's imaginative and sensitive nature, stunted by her father's system of training, is to be seen in her face and manner, as other people in the story observe. Stephen mentions her 'fine dark thinkin' eyes, and a still way' (p. 157). Harthouse is struck by her appearance on first meeting. She is the 'most remarkable girl' he has ever seen:

> She was so constrained, and yet so careless; so reserved, and yet so watchful;
> so cold and so proud, and yet so sensitively ashamed of her husband's
> braggart humility ... Utterly indifferent, perfectly self-reliant, never at
> a loss, and yet never at her ease ... and her mind apparently quite alone
> (pp. 131–2).

The last idea, that she is alone in her mind, is conveyed by the **image**, in Chapters 8 and 15 of Book I, of Louisa sitting by the fire watching the sparks and wondering, although her father has forbidden wonder. She speaks dramatically of fire, as a **symbol** of suppressed passion and dreams, in the scene with her father in Book I Chapter 15 (see Textual Analysis, Text 2).

Louisa's devotion to Tom becomes more understandable in view of the inner loneliness of her upbringing. This love is described in very physical terms when she lies on Tom's bed pleading with him to confess to her about the robbery, in Book II Chapter 8. Her reconciliation with Sissy, in Book III Chapter 1, also stresses physical contact between the two women. Such passages may hint at unhappiness in her marriage.

Louisa's speech is often **melodramatic**, especially in the scene with her father after her flight from Harthouse, in Book II Chapter 12. Her long **rhetorical** sentences and exaggerated gestures, there, would have seemed routine to an actress playing her part in a stage version in 1854, but might well trouble a modern performer. We may call such scenes unrealistic, or alternatively say that Louisa's real emotions are conveyed through a literary convention belonging to her own age (although, given Gradgrind's system, it is one that Louisa is unlikely to have known). For more about Louisa, see Themes, on Women's Lives, and Critical History, on Feminist Criticism.

MRS GRADGRIND

Gradgrind seems to have crushed his wife's personality out of her by his overassertiveness. She makes only brief appearances, often at the ends of chapters, and her talk is stumbling and usually close to nonsense. Images convey her feebleness of body and mind. She looks like 'a mere bundle of shawls' (p. 22), or like a 'transparency with not enough light behind it' (p. 23). She is totally ineffective as a mother, her failure here adding to the breakdown of normal family relations in Gradgrind's home. Her one remarkable scene is her last. Many critics have testified to the uncanny sense generated by her broken speech and invisible writing of some message of 'wonderful no-meaning' on her bed-clothes, as she dies, in Book II Chapter 9 (see Critical History, on Feminist Criticism).

SISSY JUPE

Cecilia Jupe first appears as 'Girl number twenty' in Book I Chapter 2. Here she begins her role in the **satirical** attack on Gradgrind's system of teaching. Sissy is right to get her lessons wrong. Later on she shows up M'Choakumchild's doctrinaire **utilitarian** teaching. When he asks for the first principle of Political Economics (self-interest), she replies by quoting the Golden Rule, to do as you would be done by (p. 60). The point of her failure at school, strongly brought out in Book I Chapter 9, is that the teachers are the dunces, and Sissy too wise in knowledge of the heart to learn from them.

Some characters are presented in close relation to an institution. Sissy is always associated with the circus, where she learned what horses are, rather than how to define them. Her love never falters for her father, the unsuccessful clown for whose sake she preserves for many years the soothing bottle of 'nine oils'. Sissy helps to make the circus seem a place of true human relationships, in contrast to Coketown and Gradgrind's home.

She assumes the role of mother to the younger Gradgrind children. In her guise as 'angel in the house' she corresponds to a Victorian stereotype of women who fulfil themselves at home rather than out in the men's world. She is remarkably active, however, in the later stages of the novel, befriending Rachael, helping to find Stephen, helping Tom to escape, and above all in the scene where she sends Harthouse packing, in Book III Chapter 2.

All the arts of this man of the world are lost on Sissy: 'her mind looked over and beyond him' (p. 234); 'he could as easily have changed a clear sky by looking at it in surprise, as affect her' (p. 236). It is her simplicity that defeats him; his 'looking … in surprise' with an ironically raised eyebrow means nothing to her. Critics have found this scene successful in its power to surprise and persuade us with the force of Sissy's moral superiority to a heartless man (see Language & Style; and Critical History, on Feminist Criticism).

Although Sissy is the heroine, she appears in relatively few scenes, and has no lover (a possibility Dickens raised in his plans for the novel, and decided against). She is rewarded with 'happy children' in the vision of the future in the last chapter.

STEPHEN BLACKPOOL

Stephen represents the 'Hands', and is meant to seem typical in some respects and not in others. His dignity, patience and courtesy reflect qualities Dickens reported finding among the Preston strikers during his visit there in January 1854 (see Historical Background). He shares these qualities with the indomitable Rachael, and depends on her support at crucial moments, notably when he is tempted to let his wife die, in Book I Chapter 13.

In other respects, 'Old Stephen' (so called, although only in his forties) is untypical. He is exceptionally awkward and stubborn. He antagonises not only Bounderby and the trade unionists, but also many critics of the novel. Some critics find him stupid. It is stupid to go to Bounderby for help, but this folly seems connected with Stephen's integrity. Socialists have objected to the mildness of his criticism of capitalism, as well as to his refusal to join the union. In his second scene with Bounderby, in Book II Chapter 5, he lays responsibility for reform on the bosses, and here as elsewhere he sticks to his formula that society is 'a muddle'. Other weavers would have found stronger terms than that (and so does Dickens). 'Muddle', always stubbornly repeated, is characteristic of Stephen's slow, obdurate approach to the world.

Objections to Stephen, as a 'weakness' in the novel, mostly come from critics who would have liked a more radical and practical figure in his place. Dickens was perhaps eager to calm middle-class readers by presenting a moderate, ineffectual and Christian workman, and by putting some of his own anti-union views into Stephen's speeches. Judged as an individual, however, Stephen is a consistent and, for some readers at least, likeable character. His refusal to join the union, and his insistence that he has promised Rachael not to, are typical of his stubbornness. He can be seen as a living refutation of the **utilitarian** idea that all human action is motivated by self-interest. He *would* marry the wrong woman, get himself ostracised and then fired, and fall down the shaft. Readers with a sneaking liking for Stephen may also think that he would deliver a long speech on factory abuses after being raised, near death, from a week-long ordeal at the bottom of a shaft. He is that sort of lad.

Critics sometimes compare Dickens's characters to caricatures. Some descriptions of Stephen might instead remind us of photographs. His shortsighted, attentive, concentrated look is captured as though in close-up, in Book I Chapter 12, and attributed to long hours of work 'with eyes and hands in the midst of a prodigious noise' (p. 81). Later there is an **image** of him as though in a long-distance shot, standing before the union members: 'He made a sort of reverence to them by holding up his arms, and stood for the moment in that attitude' (p. 146). That sighting catches his dignity and vulnerability.

JAMES HARTHOUSE

Harthouse is a social success in the provincial society of Coketown as a gentleman from London who has been an officer in a smart regiment and has served as a diplomat. His accent, manners, bearing and languid way of talking impress everybody there, except Sissy; but they are not meant to impress the reader.

He is frequently pictured or referred to as a devil; as Tom's 'Familiar', or evil tempter, for example (p. 171). This can be seen as another pantomime role, that of demon king, surrounded by (cigar) smoke; but Dickens probably meant us to believe that in playing with Louisa's affections, even if only to relieve his boredom, and in cynically playing with politics, Harthouse is doing the devil's work.

Dickens hated the idleness and affectation of 'gentlemen' (a term he often derided) who wasted the social advantages they obtained from birth and education. It is Harthouse's posing, as a man who must be superior because he has seen through everything and everybody, that makes him akin to Bounderby, his political ally, another egotist living behind a false social screen.

Other characters reveal themselves in his company. Tom is more whelp-like when fawning on Harthouse. Louisa grows more sympathetic as we see how the emptiness of her life puts her at his mercy. Mrs Sparsit looks more of a sycophant in his company. Sissy is most formidable, or angelic, when she outfaces him.

TOM GRADGRIND

Tom is too much of a 'donkey', his own term for himself (p. 56), to benefit from the facts to be learnt in the Gradgrind system. He learns only to seek the interests of 'number one' (p. 94), meaning himself. He does so by gambling and then stealing to pay his debts, and by exploiting his sister.

He is frequently contrasted with his sister. Harthouse immediately senses that Louisa is remarkable, a gifted woman trapped in a marriage that restricts her, and he discovers just as quickly that Tom is a 'whelp', the most contemptuous term he knows for a worthless youth. Tom has less imagination, intelligence or human sympathy than his sister, in whom these qualities have been suppressed or distorted. She believes she might have nourished his mind and heart in a different sort of home (p. 56). The new school of Fact has left him without principles, resentful, selfish and a coward.

He is more sympathetic than Bitzer because his failings arise from weakness and Bitzer's from strength. This means that Bitzer is the true disciple of the Gradgrind–Bounderby school, while Tom does, eventually, as we are told in the last chapter, die penitent.

BITZER

Bitzer and Sissy are pictured in contrasting **images** in the opening scene, where Sissy's dark hair and eyes suggest richness and warmth while his colourless appearance suggests the opposite: 'he looked as though, if he were cut, he would bleed white' (p. 12).

Bitzer is quick to learn facts; his memorised definition of a horse is spouted while she remains silent. Throughout the novel, he appears as a modern Coketowner, while she is the circus child. He is always an isolated figure, wedded to his own interests, while Sissy is always committed to helping others.

Like Tom, Bitzer means to help 'number one', but he is much cleverer and better able to advance in the world by cunning and deceit. At the bank, where he starts as a 'light porter' (allowing Dickens to pun on 'light'), he is the ally of Mrs Sparsit, sharing her views on the folly of the lower classes. He is said to fill the 'respectable office of general spy and informer' in Bounderby's service (p. 120), a phrase to be remembered when he tracks Tom down at the end. His rejection of Gradgrind's plea for mercy, and the chilling tone in which he speaks about the iron law of self-interest, at the end, is the novel's ultimate demonstration of what **utilitarian** philosophy really means (see Historical Background, on Utilitarianism). His subsequent promotion to Tom's position in the bank, in the last chapter, helps to connect Gradgrind's theories with Bounderby's business, in the structural scheme.

Bitzer certainly lacks human interest, but he is an effective **satirical** device. While Tom is made to seem human by his weakness and cowardice, the efficient Bitzer develops from a calculating boy into a mechanical man, the most up-to-date of Coketown's inventions.

RACHAEL

Rachael's saintly qualities make some critics think her unrealistic, and she is certainly unusual in her patient devotion. She admits to weakness, when she has Sissy to comfort her, after Stephen's disappearance, saying that without the other woman's friendship she would fear for her own sanity (p. 257). Her hysterical outburst, screaming and threatening to leap down the shaft, after she and Sissy find Stephen's hat beside the pit-shaft, is a credible response, given the years during which she has had to conceal her love even from Stephen. The display of long-suppressed emotion adds poignancy to his small, dying jest, later in the chapter, that they can for once walk together tonight (p. 274).

The last chapter, picturing her future life as it might appear to a stranger, is especially poignant (see comments on Book III Chapter 9, in Detailed Summaries).

MR SLEARY

Sleary is a good example of how expressive speech habits can be in Dickens. He is an unusual but eloquent speaker ('cackler'), his lisp and circus terminology adding to the charm of his speeches, once we are used to them. His 'Squire' ('Thquire'), for example, as a form of address for Gradgrind, a not-over-respectful courtesy title, acknowledges his visitor's status in the alien but necessary world of patrons, while insisting at the same time on his independence (by not saying 'sir').

The circus owner is also the spokesman for the circus and the embodiment of its spirit. Sleary is hospitable: 'What thall it be Thquire … thall it be Therry?' (p. 42); gentle, for a circus master: 'I never did a horthe a injury yet, no more than thwearing at him went', p. 44; resourceful, contriving Tom's escape; a father-figure in the extended family of the circus; and a spokesman for Dickens when he tells Gradgrind, and the reader, that 'people mutht be amuthed' (p. 292).

THEMES

FACTS & FIGURES

'My satire is against those who see facts and figures and nothing else', Dickens wrote soon after finishing *Hard Times*, 'the representatives of the wickedest and most enormous vice of the time' (letter to Charles Knight, 30 January 1855). Gradgrind insists on 'facts and nothing else' from the first page onwards; the facts of a case, in this novel, usually turn out to be statistics, as when Gradgrind discusses with Louisa whether she should marry Bounderby. Otherwise 'facts' refers to some sort of abstraction, as in Bitzer's definition of a horse. Sissy knows what a horse really is but cannot state the 'fact'. Dickens asserts that the 'enormous vice' of **utilitarian** extremists threatens to deny the entire human world by reducing it to abstractions.

The novel persistently attacks the compiling and deployment of information. The facts M'Choakumchild has ready for the little vessels in the second chapter will be murderous to all true aims of education. The 'blue books', or parliamentary reports, in Gradgrind's study are full of facts and figures, but not all this information will teach him to understand his child (p. 99). Dickens implies that they will not help anyone else either. Parliament is pictured as a refuse-heap of worthless facts, like dust or dung that politicians throw in each other's eyes.

The novel juxtaposes the frenzied pursuit of facts and figures with actual human suffering, in Stephen, in Rachael, in Louisa, in Mrs Gradgrind, which cannot, we are constantly told, be measured or statistically analysed. Dickens explicitly appeals in Book I Chapter 11, in the brief scene inside the mill where Stephen works, against trying to measure or tabulate the lives of people like him. There is an 'unfathomable mystery' in 'the meanest labouring man', he says, and pleads that we 'reserve our arithmetic for material objects' (p. 74).

It has been argued that Dickens did not understand social science, or understand the benefits it could, eventually, bring about through parliamentary reforms. Other reformers, and notably G.B. Shaw (see Critical History, on Socialist Views) have agreed with Dickens's sweeping denunciation.

The target Dickens most consistently hits is, perhaps, not an institution such as social science, but a complacent and detached tone of voice, recommending facts and figures in situations where emotion and imagination are called for instead. We hear it in the 'Fact' of the opening words of the book, and in many other passages. It was a tone of voice Dickens heard in officialdom, excusing itself, and he wrote to persuade us of its wickedness.

FANCY

One way to interpret the novel is by contrasting fact and fancy. Another contrast, between head and heart, fits in because Gradgrind equates fact with tough rationality and dismisses emotion as fanciful nonsense. While he and Bounderby are on the side of facts, the novel is all for fancy, and is indeed the very book they would most want to exclude from Coketown's library.

The theme of fancy is linked with entertainment. *Hard Times* continually draws inspiration from pantomime, represented in Sleary's Circus by acts such as Babes in the Wood and Jack the Giant-killer, and in Dickens by innumerable images and jokes directed against the humourless and unimaginative champions of fact. Almost as soon as Gradgrind has proclaimed the rule of Fact, this fanciful world takes the stage:

> Say, good M'Choakumchild. When from thy boiling store, thou shalt fill each jar
> brim full by and by, dost thou think that thou wilt always kill outright the robber
> Fancy lurking within – or sometimes only maim him and distort him! (p. 15)

M'Choakumchild has been turned into Morgiana in the tale of 'Ali Baba and the Forty Thieves' in *Arabian Nights* (and so into the old-fashioned language of the story-book, with *thou* and *thy*). She poured boiling oil into the large jars where the thieves were hiding. M'Choakumchild is eager to pour facts into the little vessels (children) and kill fancy. This last point is seriously meant, of course: fancy is to be killed in Tom and maimed in Louisa. It is characteristic of the technique of *Hard Times*, however, that Dickens has obtruded into the stern, bleak schoolroom a figure from pantomime.

Another example, where the technique is used against Bounderby, shows how the element of surprise operates in the devising of fanciful images. Bounderby taps his hat, to emphasise what he is saying, 'as if it were a tambourine'. When he has finished speaking, 'Mr Bounderby, like an oriental dancer, put his tambourine on his head' (p. 186). Street dancers in London would end their act in this way. The novel presupposes a reader who, unlike Bounderby and Gradgrind, can be amused by such flights of fancy. Dickens can always invent a surprising new **image**, and the endless unpredictability of his inventions undermines the stable world of fact. Each time this happens, the novelist's technique proves the novel's point: that the human world is more wonderful and unaccountable than all the machines in Coketown.

This element of surprise, in witty and original images, helps to distinguish fancy from fact. It is not just a matter of contrasts between **metaphorical** and literal language. The hard-fact characters use metaphor too. Gradgrind keeps saying that everything is fact, and Bounderby keeps saying that the workers' complaints all mean turtle soup. Fact is monotonous in its metaphors, while fancy is full of life and fun (for another view, see Critical History, on Deconstruction).

WOMEN'S LIVES

Coketown is run by men. Gradgrind presides over the school and is a Member of Parliament. Bounderby is prominent among the 'masters'. The trade union is for men. Even at home Gradgrind rules over his wife and children, while Bounderby thinks of Mrs Sparsit as a piece of property: 'I am the proprietor of this female' (p. 186).

There are several points, however, where the plot turns on decisions made by women. Stephen's promise to Rachael keeps him out of the union. Sissy sends Harthouse away. She and Rachael find Stephen. She hides Tom in the circus. Bounderby's bogus reputation as a self-made man collapses when his mother claims him.

The reader is likely to sympathise, moreover, with female characters. We take Sissy's side against Gradgrind and Harthouse. We feel for Louisa, not Tom, let alone Bounderby or Harthouse. Rachael's distress, when Stephen falls down the shaft, helps to make his plight poignant and not just a typical Dickensian plot device. Mrs Sparsit is most remote from the reader's sympathy when hounding Louisa, and nearest in the last chapter where she calls him a Noodle to his face.

Women also tend to be right. Rachael is right to believe in Stephen's innocence. Louisa is right to wonder. The rightness of Sissy's words subdues Harthouse. Even Mrs Gradgrind is right to think her husband has forgotten something essential.

In spite of having justice on their side, the women suffer in relative silence, amid the loud, misguided voices of men. Louisa is at a loss for words when her father asks her to marry Bounderby. Sissy cannot answer M'Choakumchild's questions. The strength of her position in her scene with Harthouse lies in her declining to argue. Mrs Gradgrind mumbles nonsense, and dies writing a wordless message. Women frequently communicate without words. When Louisa asks if Rachael is Stephen's wife, in Book II Chapter 6, 'Rachael raised her eyes, and they sufficiently answered no, and dropped again' (p. 161). Louisa catches Sissy's eye and puts her finger to her lip, in Book III Chapter 4, to say that her father must not yet be allowed to find out about Tom's guilt (p. 255). For ways in which this silencing of women has interested feminist critics, see Critical History, on Feminist Criticism.

LETTING ALONE & SELF-RELIANCE

Arguing with Bounderby, Stephen says that 'lettin' alone will never do it', that is, solve the muddle of Coketown (p. 154). The idea expressed by the French term laissez-faire (or let alone), that government should interfere in industry as little as possible, was a central principle of nineteenth-century economics. In Bounderby, Dickens attacked employers who used it as an excuse for failing to install safety measures in factories, to cover disused pit-shafts, or reduce emissions of smoke and gas. We hear how common such neglect is in Coketown in Book II Chapter 1. Bounderby tells Harthouse that factory smoke is 'the healthiest thing' for lungs, and that he means to do nothing about it (p. 130).

The words 'let be' occur in various contexts in different parts of the novel. They often seem to recommend a different 'leave alone' philosophy, one of respect for the lives of others, as in the last paragraph of all: 'Let them be!' It is often asserted that many human affairs would be better without meddling interference, especially on the part of Sabbatarians (who wanted to keep the sabbath holy by shutting down public entertainments) and Teetotal societies, which Dickens hated because he thought they were run by people with too much leisure, intent on stopping working people enjoying their free time. When Sissy and Rachael walk in the country, the larks are sarcastically said to be singing 'although it was Sunday' (p. 265), and the man who turns out to be the ablest rescue worker at the Old Hell Shaft, later in the same chapter, is drunk when the appeal for help first comes.

The doctrine of 'self-help' was connected with the idea of laissez-faire and *Hard Times* shows how this idea too could be abused. Dickens took full advantage of the Victorian spirit of free enterprise and hard work, but he opposed the influence of economists such as J.R. McCulloch (1789–1864), who wanted poor people to be told to rely only on their own efforts. Bounderby, with his talk about how the workers want luxury with no effort ('turtle soup') and his lies about his own early penury, **satirises** this false spirit of self-reliance.

Many other Coketowners are selfish or misguided individualists, seeking to isolate themselves from others. Mrs Sparsit and Bitzer, Tom and Harthouse are exclusively concerned with the interests of 'number one', and quite prepared to leave alone the problems of other people. Gradgrind views Louisa as a learning automaton. In marked contrast, we are told that Sleary's circus people have 'a special inaptitude for any kind of sharp practice, and an untiring readiness to help and pity one another' (p. 41). Sissy brings the inaptitude and readiness into Gradgrind's household, sabotaging the principles of laissez-faire and self-reliance.

TEACHING

The attack on new bearings in education in the first two chapters concentrates on excessive memorising of facts and definitions remote from children's actual experience. The newly trained M'Choakumchild is bursting with facts. Bitzer rattles off scientific properties of a horse ('Quadruped. Graminivorous. Forty teeth'), while Sissy, who lives among horses, is lost for words.

Later scenes contrast the same two children as learners of **utilitarian** economic theory. Bitzer masters this subject and is word perfect when he refuses to show mercy to Tom because it would be unscientific to do so, at the end: 'I am sure you know that the whole social system is a question of self-interest' (p. 287). Sissy is too good-hearted to succeed in the school of self-interest. She leaves school an educational failure, in Gradgrind's view, but a good woman, while Louisa, who learnt all her lessons, is disastrously immature.

Dickens and his contemporaries shared a strong belief in the influence of early schooling, and engaged in keen controversy about how it should be done. Dickens aimed to correct an imbalance, and his satire is one-sided. Some modern readers may feel there was something to be said for the Victorian requirement of thorough and exact knowledge, especially in science subjects, when children from poor homes had to be taught together in crowded classrooms.

For more on education, see Historical Background.

WORK

While Bounderby the master is a buffoon, the dignity of the working people of Coketown is stressed throughout. We hear of how some hands 'piecing together their broken intervals of leisure through many years, had mastered difficult sciences' (p. 68). Stephen can express himself clearly and coherently, but 'thousands of his compeers could talk much better than he' (p. 69). Although the trade-union delegate Slackbridge is ridiculous and sinister, the men (women not being present) listen with quiet, earnest expressions and the narrator insists on 'their honesty in the main' (p. 147).

Coketown exists only for work. *Hard Times* pleads for more leisure and entertainment. The joyless childhood of Gradgrind's children is linked with the tedium of the workers' lives: 'Is it possible, I wonder, that there was any analogy between the case of the Coketown population and the case of the little Gradgrinds?' (p. 31). The question expects the answer yes. Gradgrind's hard philosophy and Bounderby's hard business sense work together. The narrator tells us (presumably with some exaggeration) that the workers do not attend any of Coketown's many chapels, and implies that they are right to stay away while chapel-goers are eager to stop 'low singing' and 'low dancing' (p. 30).

The novel emphasises the dangers arising from pollution and factory conditions. There is 'ill-smelling dye' in the river (p. 28), and 'killing gases [are] bricked in' while Nature is bricked out, in the part of town where Stephen lives (p. 68). His loom is called 'the crashing,

smashing, tearing piece of mechanism at which he laboured' (p. 73). The
strongly worded denunciation of Coketown's ruling class at the start of
Book II refers to the factory owners' indifference to 'chopping people up
with their machinery' (p. 115). Stephen's last speech refers to Rachael's
little sister, killed by factory work. Readers of *Household Words* would
recall the article 'Ground in the Mill' (see Historical Background, on
Factory Accidents). The frequent pantomime term 'Fairy palaces', for
factories, is bitterly **ironic**.

Dickens's treatment of the trade union, and especially the figure of
Slackbridge, a crude, ranting agitator who condemns Stephen as a class
traitor, has often been adversely criticised. These scenes are balanced,
however, by the conversation between Mrs Sparsit and Bitzer in the first
chapter of Book II:

> 'What are the restless wretches doing now?' asked Mrs Sparsit.
>
> 'Merely going on in the old way, ma'am. Uniting and leaguing, and engaging to
> stand by one another.'
>
> 'It is much to be regretted,' said Mrs Sparsit, making her nose more Roman and
> her eyebrows more Coriolanian (p. 119).

In Shakespeare's play, the Roman general Coriolanus is a fierce opponent
of the political rights of the lower class, and is destroyed by his
intransigence.

ENTERTAINMENT

Coketown's library is mentioned, in Book I Chapter 8, and its literature
section with novels by Defoe and Goldsmith. They are said to be popular
with ordinary people for reasons Gradgrind cannot fathom, believing as
he does that such books have no utility. The circus has even less use,
according to this narrow view of useful knowledge and useful work.
Clowns and acrobats produce nothing. Sleary's horsy pantomimes such as
'the highly novel and laughable hippo-comedietta of the Tailor's Journey
to Brentford' (p. 18) are not serious affairs, but just fun. Dickens
explained his idea of the value of such fun, especially theatrical
entertainment of the sort serious people would call 'low', in an article on
'The Amusements of the People' (see Historical Background, on
Circuses).

Dickens was aware of affinities between Sleary's sort of showmanship and his own. We readers are, at times, present at Dickens's circus. When the dancing horse detains Bitzer at the end, it takes an appropriate revenge, circus style, for the cold definition of the opening scene. That seemed to state 'what a horse is' (p. 12), but it now appears that Bitzer still has much to learn. It is appropriate that the **utilitarian** should be defeated by the circus-master. Sleary speaks for Dickens in voicing the anti-utilitarian slogan, 'People mutht be amuthed' (p. 292).

RELIGION

The first two chapters are given biblical titles. Victorian readers would immediately recall 'the one thing needful', the title of the opening chapter, as the words of Jesus (Luke 10:42): the one thing needful is to hear his words. 'Murdering the Innocents', the next chapter title, refers to the slaughter of infants by King Herod at the time of Christ's birth (Matthew 2:16). These are the first of many **ironic** biblical allusions. When Sissy gives the 'wrong' answer to the question about economics, 'to do unto others as I would that they should do unto me' (p. 60), she is quoting the Book of Common Prayer of the Church of England, and the Bible, Matthew 7:12, and stating the core of the moral teaching of Christianity. When Gradgrind is sitting in his study on the night Louisa comes to take refuge, he is at work, 'proving something no doubt, probably, in the main, that the Good Samaritan was a bad economist' (p. 215). In the parable (Luke 10:29–37), the Good Samaritan gives money and help to a stranger in distress. Gradgrind's economic principles are the opposite of Christian charity.

There are other passages where religious phraseology and allusions to Christianity are used as bitter reproaches. At the climax of the passage sounding 'the key-note' at the beginning of Book I Chapter 5, Coketown is said to be a town 'sacred to fact', and the law of buying in the cheapest market and selling in the dearest is affirmed 'world without end, Amen', in an echo of the 'Gloria' in the Book of Common Prayer. When Gradgrind is said to have been elected to Parliament, to join the blind, deaf, dumb, lame, dead honourable gentlemen, the passage concludes, with fierce **irony**, 'Else wherefore live we in a Christian land, eighteen hundred and odd years after our Master?' (p. 96). It is repeatedly implied in this way that Christian England has forgotten its faith, and adopted a new religion of 'Fact'.

The novel offers little prospect of church or chapel fighting back. Stephen and Rachael both quote Scripture in the scene where he tells her that she has 'saved his soul alive' (p. 92). Stephen thinks of his star as the Christmas star, 'as guided to Our Saviour's home' (p. 274). We might expect that they would both be chapel-goers. Dickens's scorn for much of Victorian religiosity (which he thought unChristian) may have made him unrealistic on this point. Eighteen religious denominations are said to have built chapels in Coketown: they look like 'pious warehouses' and none of the working people attend them (p. 29). They are associated with the Sabbatarian and Teetotal societies that Dickens **satirises** throughout. Those who do attend the chapels want to make 'these people religious by main force' (p. 30), by passing laws to stop or restrict Sunday activities such as rail travel. Sissy and Louisa get into the country for their Sunday walk by train (p. 265). The Teetotal societies want stricter laws to prevent drinking. The workman who leads the effort to rescue Stephen is said to have been drunk earlier on this Sunday (p. 269). Sleary is a hard-drinker we are meant to like.

NARRATIVE TECHNIQUES

STRUCTURE

Hard Times was designed to be published in twenty weekly instalments in Dickens's magazine *Household Words*, before appearing in book form later in 1854. Dickens found the shortness of the weekly parts irksome, having become accustomed to serialisation in longer, monthly parts. He complained to a friend that 'the compression and close condensation necessary for that disjointed form of publication gave me perpetual trouble' (letter to Mrs R. Watson, 1 November 1854). Compression involved reducing and shortening the usual long passages of description and commentary. Each brief instalment had to advance the story, develop the themes, and leave the reader keen to buy the next issue. The story moves faster as a result.

The division into three 'Books' when the novel was reissued in one volume was no afterthought: it appears in Dickens's working plans. The Book titles 'Sowing', 'Reaping' and 'Garnering' would make Victorian readers remember biblical warnings about the ill-consequences of foolish actions and think of the contrast between the natural rhythms of the agricultural year and Coketown's mechanical routine. The titles suggest spring, summer and autumn, perhaps carrying the implication that harder times are yet to come.

The plot combines the story of Gradgrind's family and the story of Stephen's misfortunes, with various parallels (between Stephen's unhappy marriage and Louisa's, for example) and many connections. Tom's robbery of the bank and his putting of the blame on Stephen are crucial actions, affecting everybody. Even Mrs Pegler becomes a suspect because she was seen with Stephen on the day he lost his job. As a result of the robbery, Mrs Sparsit becomes Bounderby's house-guest and begins to spy on Harthouse and Louisa. Sissy banishes Harthouse. She and Rachael become friends. Stephen appeals to Gradgrind to clear his name. Bitzer tries to have Tom arrested after Sissy has hidden him in the circus but Sleary intervenes to let him escape. Careful plotting connects almost all the characters in the closing stages. Such a design is typical of Dickens. It is meant to show how, whatever the divisions caused by wealth and class, individuals cannot exist in isolation but depend on one another, like it or not.

Hard Times has something of the tight design of a **fable**. Like a fable it shapes the story to make moral points, in a series of **ironic** upsets. Gradgrind sows the seeds of the misery he reaps. His vigilant care for his children's upbringing leads to their ruin. He even introduces Harthouse to Coketown. His model pupil Bitzer rejects his plea for mercy by quoting Gradgrind's own theories. The circus he so despises sends him the angel Sissy, and Sleary rescues Tom. Bounderby is punished for his indifference to Stephen's broken marriage when his own marriage fails. His own mother is the undoing of the self-made man.

TIME

The story covers the events of rather more than five years. It moves in chronological order from start to finish. The passage of four years or more, taking Louisa from 'fifteen or sixteen' to about twenty, is reported in Book I Chapter 14, and a further year passes between Books I and II. The apt **personification** of Time as a great manufacturer is used for the first and longer of these interludes.

The pace of events is brisker than in many of Dickens's novels, partly because weekly serialisation required new developments in each of the twenty parts. Much of the action is presented in short dramatic scenes with frequent but brief comments. Suspense over the fates of Stephen and Tom hastens the story to its end.

There is a strong sense of topicality throughout, most obviously in the fully developed national railway system, constructed in the course of the 1840s, in the well-established trade union, and in the professionally trained schoolteachers. Obviously, the first thirteen chapters, set back five years or more, must belong to the late 1840s. Hints in the first two chapters of a much more recent date (see Historical Background) are, therefore, tricks with time, but not conspicuous ones. Victorian novels often begin a generation or so back in time to allow characters to grow up and pass into middle age. The contemporary setting in *Hard Times* means that the accounts of later lives in the last chapter are glimpses into the future on the part of the narrator.

POINT OF VIEW

The narrator is **omniscient**, able to look back into Louisa's memory or forwards into the future, and to report on Stephen's dream and Mrs Sparsit's giant staircase. He is reliable about events, although readers need not agree with all his comments.

This omniscience is restricted in many scenes, presented from the **point of view** of one or more of the characters. We follow Stephen's point of view, for example, from his first appearance to the night he is tempted to let his wife die. This restriction helps with suspense, especially in the closing stages. We share the anxiety of Rachael and Sissy about what has become of Stephen, in Book III. The narrator knows, but withholds the surprise of his discovery. It is from the point of view of Sissy and Louisa that we observe Gradgrind's growing suspicion of Tom's guilt. There are, however, few dramatic surprises. It is easy to guess who Mrs Pegler is. Frequent changes of point of view, from one character to another, prevent the emergence of any single hero or heroine.

The earliest readers probably thought of the narrator as Dickens. In *Household Words*, his name appeared at the head of every page. Modern readers are more likely to be aware of several voices in the narrative. Sometimes we are listening to a Coketowner who has known the place for years. Sometimes the comments are those of an outraged outsider – someone like Dickens on a visit to the North. Occasionally we are teased by the author in the background. Spying on Harthouse and Louisa, Mrs Sparsit is too far away to overhear, we are told; 'but what they said was this' (p. 204). Sometimes an authoritative, often angry voice breaks in, as in Book II Chapter 6, when Stephen and Rachael part, and Dickens seems to address groups of his fellow-Victorians directly with words of warning and denunciation: 'Utilitarian economists, skeletons of schoolmasters, Commissioners of Fact ...' (p. 165). At many points, for those who have read other novels by Dickens, the story-teller's blend of indignation, amusement and gusto also sounds very Dickensian.

LANGUAGE & STYLE

Dickens's source for dialect was *A View of the Lancashire Dialect* (1746) by 'Tim Bobbin' (pseudonym of John Collier). Many dialect forms can be guessed from the context: nouns include *brigg* for 'bridge', *chilt* for 'child' and *een* for 'eyes'. Stephen clips off the ends of words, saying *fra* for 'from' and *ha* for 'have'. Spellings sometimes indicate his pronunciation: *ett'n* for 'eaten', and *owd* for 'old'. Some forms are known to anyone who has ever heard northern English spoken: *nowt* ('nothing'), *nobbut* ('only') and *haply* or *happen* ('perhaps'). Grammatical irregularities, such as the double negative and omission of articles, are common to many English dialects. There is just enough Lancashire to give a northern flavour to the speech of Stephen and Rachael, and to add freshness and vigour to some of their speeches. Here is Stephen before Bounderby, talking himself out of his job: 'and look how mills is awlus [always] a goin, and how they never works us no nigher [nearer] to ony dis'ant object – ceptin awlus, Death (p. 153). We have just learnt the odd form *awlus*, when we hear it at the climax of the sentence.

Dickens did some research into circus jargon (see Historical Background). Some of Sleary's terms convey circus ways of thinking, as when he says that Sissy's father has *morrithed* ('morrised'), or skipped away like a morris-dancer. *Cackler*, Sleary's word for a clown with a speaking part, seems to have amused Dickens by making merely verbal entertainment sound inferior – nothing to bareback-riding or acrobatics.

Dickens was a gifted cackler: actor, mimic, and novelist with amazing flair for reproducing odd varieties of speech. It is a mark of Gradgrind's and Bounderby's narrow-mindedness that they cannot enjoy the unusual talk to be heard among Sleary's people. They both have a crude concept of language, summarised when Bounderby says he always calls a post a post (p. 110). The circus scenes show how unpredictable language is. Bounderby clashes with 'Cupid', a circus boy with a sharp tongue:

> 'Queer sort of company too for a man who has raised himself.'
>
> 'Lower yourself, then!' retorted Cupid. 'Oh Lord! if you've raised yourself so high as all that comes to, let yourself down a bit.'
>
> 'This is a very obtrusive lad!' said Mr Gradgrind. (p. 37)

Raising oneself has a different meaning in the circus from the social sense. Bounderby is 'on the Tight-Jeff', says Cupid (Master Kidderminster, out of the ring), that is to say up on the tight-rope and liable to fall off. The boy's impudence is matched by the playful insubordination of language.

Individual speech habits help create character. Bounderby's habit of speaking of himself in the third person ('Josiah Bounderby of Coketown') suggests that he has lost touch with reality. He is always interrupting and giving orders ('Stop a bit!') and endlessly repeating his stale jokes ('turtle soup'). Slackbridge and Sleary also have distinctive **idiolects**. In Slackbridge, Dickens ridicules the phraseology of windbag orators by packing too many 'friends', 'slaves' and 'grinding despotisms' together: 'Oh my friends and fellow countrymen, the slaves of an iron-handed and a grinding despotism' (p. 141). In Sleary's speeches, the remorseless substitution of every sibilant with *th* – more than thirty lisps in the twelve lines of his last speech at the end of Book I Chapter 6 – makes it a game to decode him. It also suggests the asthmatic effort of speaking, in contrast to Slackbridge's mechanical glibness, and adds a personal weight to his assertions about 'amuthement'.

Not all the characters speak so consistently. Harthouse is usually offhand, lazily affecting subjectless sentences: 'Has resources of her own?', 'Formed his daughter on his own model?' (p. 139). When he tries to seduce Louisa, his language fills with artificial formulas, such as saying he has fallen prostrate under her foot (p. 212). Louisa's remark about letting Tom cut Bounderby's kiss out of her cheek with his penknife (p. 28) sounds genuinely childish; but her speeches to her father at the end of Book II are in the style of stage **melodrama** (see Characterisation).

The narrator adds to the novel's **polyphony** – its variety of voices. Some judgements are crisp: 'he was a good power-loom weaver and a man of perfect integrity' (p. 69). In other passages Dickens enjoyed himself. Here is his commentary on Gradgrind's election to Parliament:

> one of the respected members for ounce weights and measures, one of the representatives of the multiplication table, one of the deaf honourable gentlemen, dumb honourable gentlemen, blind honourable gentlemen, lame honourable gentlemen, dead honourable gentlemen, to every other consideration. Else wherefore live we in a Christian land, eighteen hundred and odd years after our Master? (p. 96)

Dickens often relies on repetition. Here he mocks repetitious political speeches, full of the title 'honourable gentlemen' that MPs use of one another. Unlike much political speechifying, Dickens's style expects us to pay close attention: 'dead' brings the list of politicians' shortcomings to a climax. Then 'dead ... *to*' turns all the adjectives into **metaphors**: politicians are deaf, blind and dead to everything except their obsession with statistics ('multiplication table'). The **rhetorical question** in the last sentence is typical of **ironic** references throughout the novel to England as a Christian country where Christianity is widely ignored (see Themes, on Religion).

The narrative is constantly inventive with metaphors. Oddly applied **epithets** spice the **satire**: 'his metallurgical Louisa' (p. 19); Mrs Sparsit has a 'highly connected back' (p. 214). Many images are apt and surprising: the Coketown evergreens are sprinkled with dust 'like untidy snuff-takers' (p. 167). Others are effectively simple. Rachael ignores all suspicions about Stephen, 'throwing off distrust as a rock throws off the sea' (p. 254).

Dickens's prose always repays attention. His verbless sentences, for example are like stage directions. They catch the tension when Louisa and her father are sitting together in Book I Chapter 15: 'Silence between them. The deadly-statistical clock very hollow. The distant smoke very black and heavy' (p. 100).

At emotional moments, the narrator **apostrophises** the characters like a **chorus,** as when Sissy's hand falls on Louisa's neck: 'Let it lie there, let it lie' (p. 227).

For more on **imagery** see: Themes, on Fancy; Textual Analysis, Text 1; and the following section.

IMAGERY & SYMBOLISM

Dickens often pictures people as things and brings objects to life. Bounderby and Gradgrind resemble features of their houses. Gradgrind's is 'a great square house, with a heavy portico darkening the principal windows, as its master's heavy brows overshadowed his eyes' (p. 17). The first page of the book stresses Gradgrind's squareness ('square coat, square legs, square shoulders'), implying that he is as rigid as his own conceptions, the embodiment of fact. His house corresponds, as though he has imposed himself on it. The capital letters on the plaque on Bounderby's front door are 'very like himself', bold and assertive (p. 74). Physical appearances are signs of what people are like.

All Coketown signifies its own nature. Its furnaces, gaslights, steam-engines, looms, chimneys, warehouses, narrow streets, railways and above all its suffocating smoke convey its dangerous, violent, ugly, monotonous, stifling way of life. It threatens to turn people into servants for machines, so that people call men 'Hands'; or into machines, so that Tom, caught by his father at the circus, 'gave himself up to be taken home like a machine' (p. 19).

The novel illustrates the truth of its own argument: that the human mind is imaginative, first, and able to store facts and do sums, afterwards. **Images** are drawn from the most fanciful sorts of literature, including fairy stories and nursery rhymes. Even the hard-fact men cannot avoid talking in such terms. Bounderby speaks of the mysterious old country-woman 'flying into town on a broomstick' (p. 187), though he cannot guess what witchcraft Mrs Pegler is going to work on him. His house is called 'the red brick castle of the giant Bounderby' (p. 149). Images of this sort suggest a pantomime version of the story, where Bounderby is a giant, Mrs Sparsit a witch, Louisa and Tom the Babes in the Wood, Gradgrind an ogre, Harthouse a demon, Sissy a guardian angel, Louisa a sleeping beauty, and so on. This playful version of Coketown's grim reality is connected with the holiday world of the circus. Babes in the Wood is part of Sleary's company's repertoire, and Tom ends up in a minor role in Jack the Giant-killer. It is **ironic** as well as fanciful. 'Fairy palaces', the name so often used for factories because they look pretty from passing trains when lit by gas at night, is a most sarcastic term.

The contrast between Coketown and the circus is central and **symbolic**. Machines are contrasted with horses, weary labourers with daredevil riders and acrobats. Division and conflict in Coketown contrasts with community in the circus. Gradgrind sees the circus as a symbol of dangerous, corrupting Fancy. His dependence on Sleary at the end is a symbolic submission.

Many images and patterns of imagery recur throughout, so that the novel has seemed to many modern critics a symbolic and poetic work. The comparison of steam engines driving pistons to elephants' heads, and the drifting smoke to serpents is often repeated after its first introduction in Book I Chapter 5. The elephants 'in a state of melancholy madness' become a symbol of all that Stephen means by 'muddle'. The open shaft into which he falls, known as the Old Hell Shaft, is easily seen as another symbol of the mess that rapid unrestrained industrial development has brought about. Colours, and especially darkness and light, are contrasted. Sissy's lustrous dark hair and eyes and Bitzer's unnatural lightness convey her warmth and liveliness, and his bloodless servitude to fact. Images of light and dark run all through the novel, and are used in various ways. Red is associated with anger in Bounderby, with blushing in Sissy, and with fire. (For Juliet McMaster's essay on colour symbolism in *Hard Times*, see Critical History.) For fire as a symbol, see Textual Analysis, Text 2.

Other recurring images include the poorly lit transparency, for Mrs Gradgrind, and the staircase of social downfall, which Mrs Sparsit hopes to see Louisa descend. Tom's tearing of the rosebuds, while talking to Harthouse in Book II Chapter 7, makes a quiet, moving comment on the waste of his life and Louisa's. The bottle of 'nine oils' which Sissy always keeps ready for her father's return is a small and effective token of her loving and soothing role.

PART FOUR

TEXTUAL ANALYSIS

TEXT 1   (from **BOOK I CHAPTER 5 PAGES** 28–9)

Coketown, to which Messrs Bounderby and Gradgrind now walked, was a triumph of fact; it had no greater taint of fancy in it than Mrs Gradgrind herself. Let us strike the key-note, Coketown, before pursuing our tune.

It was town of red brick, or of brick that would have been red if the smoke and ashes had allowed it; but, as matters stood it was a town of unnatural red and black like the painted face of a savage. It was a town of machinery and tall chimneys, out of which interminable serpents of smoke trailed themselves for ever and ever, and never got uncoiled. It had a black canal in it, and a river that ran purple with ill-smelling dye, and vast piles of building full of windows where there was a rattling and a trembling all day long, and where the piston of the steam-engine worked monotonously up and down, like the head of an elephant in a state of melancholy madness. It contained several large streets all very like one another, and many small streets still more like one another, inhabited by people equally like one another, who all went in and out at the same hours, with the same sound upon the same pavements, to do the same work, and to whom every day was the same as yesterday and tomorrow, and every year the counterpart of the last and the next.

These attributes of Coketown were in the main inseparable from the work by which it was sustained; against them were to be set off, comforts of life which found their way all over the world, and elegancies of life which made, we will not ask how much of the fine lady, who could scarcely bear to hear the place mentioned. The rest of its features were voluntary, and they were these.

You saw nothing in Coketown but what was severely workful. If the members of a religious persuasion built a chapel there – as the members of eighteen religious persuasions had done – they made it a pious warehouse of red brick, with sometimes (but this only in highly ornamented examples) a bell in a bird-cage on the top of it. The solitary exception was the New Church; a stuccoed edifice with a square steeple over the door, terminating in four short pinnacles like florid wooden legs. All the public inscriptions in the town were painted alike, in severe characters of black and white. The jail might have been the infirmary, the infirmary might have been the jail, the town-hall might have been either, or both, or anything else, for anything that appeared to the contrary in the graces of their construction. Fact, fact, fact, everywhere in the material aspect of the town; fact, fact, fact, everywhere in the immaterial. The M'Choakumchild school was all fact, and the school of design was all fact, and the relations between master and man were all fact, and everything was fact between the lying-in [maternity] hospital and the cemetery, and what you couldn't state in figures, or show to be purchaseable in the cheapest market and saleable in the dearest, was not, and never should be, world without end, Amen.

A town so sacred to fact, and so triumphant in its assertion, of course got on well? Why no, not quite well. No? Dear me!

We have already heard (in Chapter 3) about 'a great town ... called Coketown in the present faithful guidebook' (p. 17). Preston, a big cotton town, had been much in the news (see Historical Background, on Industrial Background), but Victorian readers who knew the Midlands and north of England would probably take Coketown as the fictional name for a typical manufacturing centre. Details in this passage would fit many such places, all consuming large amounts of coke, although the style is far from that of an ordinary journalist's report.

The opening chapters have established the deadly use Gradgrind makes of 'Fact'. He and Bounderby are now on their way to meet Sleary's people, who are to represent fancy, but first we are given this grotesquely fanciful vision of Coketown as a citadel of fact. Coketown is the key-note of the tune, the clue to the whole story. Its physical filth, the first impression here and an overwhelming one throughout, is not just a matter of soot and ashes, but a **symbol** of the social mess it is in.

The 'painted face of a savage', like Tom's painted face at the circus in Book III, conveys a sense of shameful incongruity; Tom is ashamed to show his face. The canal is black and the river purple with the pollution that has disfigured a great town (and the surrounding countryside, as we learn later). A sense of the unnatural is enhanced in the second paragraph. Smoke snakes across the sky, but these are not live but diabolical serpents that 'trailed themselves for ever and ever and never got uncoiled'. The steam engine and piston rise and fall like the head and trunk of a nightmarish elephant, melancholy mad. The **image** gives a strong sense of something powerful, dangerous and out of place, working away on its own.

The rise and fall of the elephant's head is also monotonous, and this aspect of Coketown is the next to be stressed. The last long sentence has a pattern and rhythm that suggest dreary repetition:

every day	the same	as yesterday
every year	the counterpart	of the last
		and the next

Repetition, in 'same hours', 'same pavements', 'same work', evokes the monotony of lives spent between factory and home. Gradgrind's theory and Bounderby's practice, it is implied, have reduced people's lives to a dull, mechanical regularity.

Attention now turns to those responsible for this unnatural scene. Of course, Coketown is in business, and has to work for its living. A brief acknowledgement of the export of cheap, mass-produced cottonwear ('comforts of life') all over the world, which made Lancashire such a valuable part of the British economy, is followed by a reference to luxury items made for rich customers in the South, who would not care to hear Coketown's name mentioned. The sense of a divided society is continued in the next paragraph, which turns to 'voluntary' features of Coketown, that is to say not required by making and selling cotton goods. Eighteen religious sects (perhaps not much of an exaggeration) have divided Christianity among them; master and man are divided too (and only masters go to the chapels).

The penultimate paragraph builds up to a resounding climax. The theme is the rule of 'fact', meaning ugly, soulless, inhuman dedication to profit. 'Fact, fact, fact' is not what Gradgrind thought he meant in the first chapter, but Dickens's bitterly **ironic** interpretation of Gradgrindery. 'Fact' means functional architecture, all buildings looking alike (or, if not, ridiculous). 'Fact' means deadly religion, education and industrial relations. 'Fact' is the true religion of Coketown ('a town so sacred to fact'), and the economic creed of **utilitarians** such as Bitzer (who cites the law of buying in the cheapest market and selling in the dearest at the end of the story) is substituted for the Gloria of the Church of England's Book of Common Prayer: 'Glory be to the Father, and to the Son, and to the Holy Ghost: As it was in the Beginning, is now and ever shall be: world without end: Amen'. Such scathing quotation and allusion to religious language is a common feature of *Hard Times*, and implies that this avowedly Christian country has lost its faith (see Themes, on Religion).

The next two lines change the tone, after this soaring crescendo, to one of quiet irony, in a style of commentary the novelist E.M. Forster (1879–1970) was to develop into a fine art half a century later: 'not quite well. No? Dear me!'. Although the tone changes, the point of the **satire** is reinforced, in the unremitting manner of the novel as a whole. The key-note is Coketown, and Coketown is a disgrace.

TEXT 2   (from **BOOK I CHAPTER 15 PAGES 102–3**)

'Louisa,' returned her father, 'it appears to me that nothing can be plainer. Confining yourself rigidly to Fact, the question of Fact you state to yourself is: Does Mr Bounderby ask me to marry him? Yes, he does. The sole remaining question then is: Shall I marry him? I think nothing can be plainer than that.'

'Shall I marry him?' repeated Louisa, with great deliberation.

'Precisely. And it is satisfactory to me, as your father, my dear Louisa, to know that you do not come to the consideration of that question with the previous habits of mind, and habits of life, that belong to many young women.'

'No, father,' she returned, 'I do not.'

'I now leave you to judge for yourself,' said Mr Gradgrind. 'I have stated the case, as such cases are usually stated among practical minds; I have stated it, as the case of your mother and myself was stated in its time. The rest, my dear Louisa, is for you to decide.'

From the beginning, she had sat looking at him fixedly. As he now leaned back in his chair, and bent his deep-set eyes upon her in his turn, perhaps he might have seen one wavering moment in her, when she was impelled to throw herself upon his breast, and give him the pent-up confidences of her heart. But, to see it, he must have overleaped at a bound the artificial barriers he had for many years been erecting, between himself and all those subtle essences of humanity which will elude the utmost cunning of algebra until the last trumpet ever to be sounded shall blow even algebra to wreck. The barriers were too many and too high for such a leap. With his unbending, utilitarian, matter-of-fact face, he hardened her again, and the moment shot away into the plumbless depths of the past, to mingle with all the lost opportunities that are drowned there.

Removing her eyes from him, she sat so long looking silently towards the town, that he said, at length: 'Are you consulting the chimneys of the Coketown works, Louisa?'

'There seems to be nothing there, but languid and monotonous smoke. Yet when the night comes, Fire bursts out, father!' she answered, turning quickly.

'Of course I know that, Louisa. I do not see the application of the remark.' To do him justice he did not, at all.

She passed it away with a slight motion of her hand, and concentrating her attention upon him again, said, 'Father, I have often thought that life is very short.' – This was so distinctly one of his subjects, that he interposed:

'It is short, no doubt, my dear. Still, the average duration of human life is proved to have increased of late years. The calculations of various life assurance and annuity offices, among other figures which cannot go wrong, have established the fact.'

'I speak of my own life, father.'

'O indeed? Still,' said Mr Gradgrind, 'I need not point out to you, Louisa, that it is governed by the laws which govern lives in the aggregate.'

'While it lasts, I would wish to do the little I can, and the little I am fit for. What does it matter!'

Mr Gradgrind seemed rather at a loss to understand the last four words; replying, 'How, matter? What, matter, my dear?'

'Mr Bounderby,' she went on in a steady, straight way, without regarding this, 'asks me to marry him. The question I have to ask myself is, shall I marry him? That is so, father, is it not? You have told me so, father. Have you not?'

'Certainly, my dear.'

'Let it be so.'

This scene takes place in Thomas Gradgrind's study, where the new member of Parliament settles social questions by tabulating statistics. The pervading **irony** is that the man who settles big social questions cannot communicate with his favourite child. In *Bleak House*, the novel before *Hard Times*, there is a philanthropist called Mrs Jellyby, who is so busy with far-away schemes to benefit mankind that she neglects her own family. Gradgrind has made the same mistake.

This scene illustrates the significance of tone of voice throughout the novel. Gradgrind's tone reflects his state of mind. He has no notion of what is going on in Louisa's mind. Passing on Bounderby's proposal of marriage seems to him a straightforward matter, all the more so because Louisa has been schooled to avoid sentiment as something silly. His tone is businesslike and pedantic. He speaks, as though in a parliamentary committee, of 'practical minds', meaning his and hers. 'I need not point out to you, Louisa' sounds dry but not unkind, as though he were her tutor. The commentary mimics this precise and detached style of speech: 'This was so distinctly one of his subjects that he interposed'. Setting out the proposal of marriage as a sum does not quite make sense; but he is quick, when the chance comes, to turn the conversation to statistics on 'the average duration of human life', a startlingly abstract response, even for him, to Louisa's urgent reference to her own future.

In these mild lines of dialogue and comment, a cruel drama develops. It is more poignant because Gradgrind is not a monster like Bounderby. He is proud of Louisa. He commends her for having risen above the common habits of mind of young women of her age. He actually believes he has made her into a purely rational being, while she sits before him on the brink of an emotional outburst he cannot begin to suspect. His ludicrous and pathetic wrongheadedness is conveyed indirectly but forcefully through his quiet, judicious, irrelevant remarks.

It would be unlike Dickens, however, to leave everything to **irony** The narrator makes one direct protest, when we are told of the barriers Gradgrind has erected 'between himself and all those subtle essences of humanity which will elude the utmost cunning of algebra until the last trumpet ever to be sounded shall blow even algebra to wreck'. This **image** of the wreck of algebra (including all logic and calculation) by the angel's trumpet at the end of time openly asserts Christian belief, elsewhere often alluded to in ironic asides, in the absolute, immeasurable value of human life.

This sentence is poetic both in the image of algebra's end and in the rhythm, which is close to that of **blank verse**:

> The last trumpet ever to be sounded
> Shall blow even algebra to wreck.

Some readers find this rolling cadence overinsistent, and unsuitable in prose.

Louisa's words about the smoke, and fire bursting out, use the **symbol** of fire to suggest everything unpredictable and beyond measure in human life, but this appeal to her father is too poetic for him to understand. Symbolism is as alien as a foreign language to him. The philosophy that has crippled his imagination and sympathy is explicitly mentioned, for once, in this scene, when Louisa is on the verge of breaking down and showing her emotions: 'with his unbending, utilitarian, matter-of-fact face, he hardened her again'. It has crippled her, too, through the lifelong hardening influence that now makes it impossible for her to express her feelings or resist his will.

Louisa was pictured as a child sitting by the fire and watching the sparks and ashes while wondering about her future, in Chapter 8 ('Never Wonder'). At the end of Chapter 14, 'The Great Manufacturer', she is seen again, on the eve of the present scene, watching the fires of Coketown's furnaces in the distant night-sky from her front door, and gazing into her own fireplace, 'as she tried to discover what kind of woof Old Time … would weave' (p. 98). Fire is connected with her quiet times of inward (forbidden) wondering, therefore, but her words 'Fire bursts out, father!' suggest the dramatic release of a passionate force from the dull everyday existence represented by the smoke. A later passage reads like a comment on this moment when Louisa comes nearest to rebelling against her father's rule. This is when she meets Sissy again at the start of Book III: 'A dull anger that she should be seen in her distress … smouldered within her like an unwholesome fire. All closely imprisoned forces rend and destroy (p. 227). In failing to understand Louisa's 'Fire bursts out, father!', Gradgrind has ignored a warning. He is insensitive not only to figurative language (as he shows in his little touch of sarcasm about her consulting the chimneys), but also to her tone of voice, so different in its urgent direct appeal ('father!') to the flat tone she falls back into when she gives her consent, 'Let it be so'.

Some readers may regret that the second confrontation between father and daughter in this study, when Louisa flees from Harthouse at the end of Book II, is so **melodramatic**. Comparison of the two scenes shows how effective this first one is in its awkward silences, concentrated staring, and missed opportunities, and in its apt wording, such as 'the plumbless depths of the past', where 'plumbless' mocks Gradgrind, who always wants to measure everything. Rereading, we are likely to be struck by the **dramatic irony** in this first encounter, in the words 'satisfactory to me as your father', for example. The scene does prepare, however, for her later storm of passionate accusations against her father, when 'the feelings long suppressed broke loose' (p. 219), and for their reconciliation in Book III. In this scene some readers may begin to feel sorry, not only for Louisa, but for Thomas Gradgrind as well.

TEXT **3**   (from **BOOK III CHAPTER 3 PAGES 243–4**)

The blustrous Bounderby crimsoned and swelled to such an extent on hearing these words, that he seemed to be, and probably was, on the brink of a fit. With his very ears a bright purple shot with crimson, he pent up his indignation, however, and said:

'You'd like to keep her here for a time?'

'I – I had intended to recommend, my dear Bounderby, that you should allow Louisa to remain here on a visit, and be attended by Sissy (I mean of course Cecilia Jupe), who understands her, and in whom she trusts.'

'I gather from all this, Tom Gradgrind,' said Bounderby, standing up with his hands in his pockets, 'that you are of opinion that there's what people call some incompatibility between Loo Bounderby and myself.'

'I fear there is at present a general incompatibility between Louisa, and – and – almost all the relations in which I have placed her,' was her father's sorrowful reply.

'Now, look you here, Tom Gradgrind,' said Bounderby the flushed, confronting him with his legs wide apart, his hands deeper in his pockets, and his hair like a hayfield wherein his windy anger was boisterous. 'You have had your say; I am going to say mine. I am a Coketown man. I am Josiah Bounderby of Coketown. I know the bricks of this town, and I know the works of this town, and I know the chimneys of this town, and I know the smoke of this town, and I know the Hands of this town. I know 'em all pretty well. They're real. When a man tells me anything about imaginative qualities, I always tell that man, whoever he is, that I know what he means. He means turtle-soup and venison, with a gold spoon, and that he wants to be set up with a coach and six. That's what your daughter wants. Since you are of opinion that she ought to have what she wants, I recommend you to provide it for her. Because, Tom Gradgrind, she will never have it from me.'

'Bounderby,' said Mr Gradgrind, 'I hoped, after my entreaty, you would have taken a different tone.'

'Just wait a bit,' retorted Bounderby, 'you have said your say, I believe. I heard you out; hear me out, if you please. Don't make yourself a spectacle of unfairness as well as inconsistency, because, although I am sorry to see Tom Gradgrind reduced to his present position, I should be doubly sorry to see him brought so low as that. Now, there's an incompatibility of some sort or other, I am given to understand by you, between your daughter and me. I'll give *you* to understand, in reply to that, that there unquestionably is an incompatibility of the first magnitude – to be summed up in this – that your daughter don't properly know her husband's merits, and is not impressed with such a sense as would become her, by George! of the honour of his alliance. That's plain speaking, I hope.'

'Bounderby,' urged Mr Gradgrind, 'this is unreasonable.'

'Is it?' said Bounderby. 'I am glad to hear you say so. Because when Tom Gradgrind with his new lights [opinions], tells me that what I say is unreasonable, I am convinced at once it must be devilish sensible. With your permission I am going on. You know my origin; and you know that for a good many years of my life I didn't want a shoeing-horn, in consequence of not having a shoe. Yet you may believe or not, as you think proper, that there are ladies – born ladies – belonging to families – Families! – who next to worship the ground I walk on.'

He discharged this, like a Rocket, at his father-in-law's head.

This passage is a good example of how Bounderby is presented by means of external appearance, beginning with the recurring epithet 'blustrous', and the recurring **image** of him swelling, reddening and threatening to explode. Soon afterwards the unruly hair that seems to blow in the wind of his anger, is mentioned again, and the passage ends with his launching of a 'Rocket' of **rhetoric,** perhaps a reference to George Stephenson's famous locomotive, since Bounderby is a man of the new railway age. He has just rushed back to Coketown by rail, having heard from Mrs Sparsit of Louisa's flight.

Bounderby is unlikely to show any sympathy for his wife or her father; unlike Gradgrind, he is the sort of comic character who does not change. Bounderby usually talks in the style of a public speech, even in private. Addressing his old friend and father-in-law, he begins 'I am a Coketown man', as though before an audience of strangers. 'I am Josiah Bounderby of Coketown' is typical of his ceaseless propaganda on his own behalf: he is the famous self-made man and leading citizen. He talks throughout as though in a meeting, and in phrases he has obviously used many times before. We know we shall soon hear about early poverty ('not having a shoe'), Mrs Sparsit ('Families!' – only aristocratic ones deserve the name) and plain-speaking ('the honour of his alliance').

His remarks about turtle soup and Coketown's smoke are equally predictable, and funny, but there is an additional dramatic point here. Gradgrind is a changed man, and his penance is going to consist partly in hearing his own arguments (notably, later from Bitzer) used against him. Here Bounderby uses the rule of fact to reject Gradgrind's plea for mercy to Louisa. Bricks and smoke are real, he says, matters of fact, but imaginative qualities mean only one thing. Once again, Gradgrind hears about the turtle soup and its accompaniments, but this time the formula is directed against him and his daughter (against Dickens, too, and the reader, if a believer in 'imaginative qualities'). Louisa is no better than the Hands, if she presumes to defy her husband.

Some readers may hesitate over a difficulty here, which arises in most of Bounderby's scenes and in connection with Dickens's comic scoundrels throughout his work. Bounderby is meant to be despicable. A Victorian might call him uncouth and monstrously egotistical; a modern reader might call him **patriarchal** in his assumption that wives like workmen must obey their masters. But the phrase about turtle soup and venison is funny because it is predictable. A common type of humour arises in just this way. Such a man might be unendurable in life but the character probably gets a smile. It could be said on Dickens's behalf, however, that men talking like Bounderby in actual life would henceforth sound ridiculous to readers of *Hard Times*. Since pride goes before a fall, this scene prepares for Bounderby's downfall, two chapters later, when Mrs Pegler puts a stop to his boasting.

Gradgrind's change of heart is taking place at this stage of the novel. It is noticeable that although he has learnt about 'the wisdom of the heart', and is more understanding than before, he remains unrealistically high-minded. In expecting Bounderby not to be 'unreasonable', he shows the same idealistic expectation as in earlier scenes. His precise, courteous speech, and his reproach, are a contrast to Bounderby's blunt bullying, when he says he had hoped that 'after my entreaties, you would have taken a different tone'. Thomas Gradgrind has learnt much, but nothing about his son-in-law. This consistency in Gradgrind's characterisation makes the change of heart more credible.

The use of names and styles of address is of interest throughout *Hard Times*. Bounderby's 'Tom Gradgrind', used in the third person in the man's presence, is a mark of bluff northern manners ('Tom Gradgrind for a bluff, independent manner of speaking – as if someone were always endeavouring to bribe him with immense sums to say Thomas, and he wouldn't', p. 49). It is part of his indifference to personal relations not to say 'Tom' or 'Gradgrind'. Bounderby's impoliteness is of the heart. He has known Gradgrind a long time, but he has no friends. He is equally impersonal elsewhere in speaking of Louisa as 'Tom Gradgrind's daughter'. Gradgrind, who began by saying 'girl number twenty', and has long said 'Jupe', shows his change of heart when he slips into saying 'Sissy', for once, a sign of his new awareness of her as a person.

PART FIVE

BACKGROUND

CHARLES DICKENS'S LIFE & WORK

Charles John Huffam Dickens was born at Portsmouth in 1812, the son of a clerk. His family soon moved to London; the city was to fascinate him all his life. As a child he was a keen reader of fiction, including eighteenth-century classics such as *Robinson Crusoe* and the *Arabian Nights*. He also delighted in plays and magic-lantern shows.

A catastrophe occurred when he was just twelve. His father was imprisoned for debt, and he was sent out to work in Warren's Blacking Factory, a humiliation that he never forgot. He was to conceal this short period of his life even from his wife and children, revealing it only to his close friend and biographer John Forster.

After a few months, his father was released and he returned to school, leaving at the age of fifteen to become an office boy. He learnt shorthand and became a journalist. In the early 1830s he was a parliamentary reporter. He began to publish sketches and stories in magazines, wandering London in search of material. His first book was a collection of these pieces, *Sketches by Boz* (1836), 'Boz' having been his childhood nickname.

In 1829 Dickens fell in love with Maria Beadnell, but her family did not permit them to marry. He married Catherine Hogarth in 1836. They had many children, but the marriage was in difficulties by 1854, when he wrote *Hard Times*, with its plea for liberal divorce laws, and there was a formal separation in 1858. In 1857, Dickens had met and fallen in love with a young actress, Ellen Ternan, an influence in his later years. There was no open scandal.

Dickens's first novel, *The Pickwick Papers* (1836), made him famous. His friend and rival W.M. Thackeray (1811–63) said that Dickens 'took his place calmly at the head of the whole tribe [of writers], and kept it'. From then on, he was always a public figure. He campaigned for schools for poor children, free libraries in working-class cities such as Manchester and Preston, and many other causes. He founded and edited the journal *Household Words* from 1850, followed after 1859 by *All the Year Round*. As a journalist he travelled widely, visiting Preston during the cotton-workers' strike there, shortly before beginning *Hard Times* (see Historical Background, on Industrial Relations).

He visited America in 1842 and again in 1867. He also spent periods in Italy and France (where he wrote much of *Hard Times*). He was a keen amateur actor; contemporaries agreed that he might have made a successful career as a professional. From 1858, he gave a series of dramatic readings from his work, in various parts of Britain and in America. The strain of these readings may have hastened his death in 1870, at the age of fifty-eight.

No English writer ever made such an impact on contemporary readers. His funeral saw an extraordinary display of public grief. Preaching the funeral-sermon in Westminster Abbey, Professor Benjamin Jowett (1817–93) said of him that 'no one was ever so much beloved or so much mourned'.

His literary work

Dickens was a prolific writer. He published fourteen novels and left another, *The Mystery of Edwin Drood*, unfinished at his death. He also wrote Christmas stories, including *A Christmas Carol* (1843), tales, plays, travel books, articles for his own journals, speeches, and many thousands of letters. The five novels he wrote between *The Pickwick Papers* in 1836 and *Barnaby Rudge* in 1841 made his reputation as a comic genius with a huge cast of vivid characters, many of them known to an even wider audience through readings and dramatisations.

He was not always consistently successful. When sales of the monthly instalments of *Martin Chuzzlewit* (1843) declined, he sent his protagonist Martin to America to revive them. He cared intensely about his readership, not only for financial reasons. He had a dramatist's sense of his public as an audience. All his novels first appeared as serials, which increased his awareness of readers following the story over the months, rather like a television audience today. Serialisation also brought technical problems (especially in *Hard Times*, published weekly, see Structure), and the need for complicated plots with continual mystery and suspense.

Twentieth-century critics have admired the later novels for their greater artistry and exacting scrutiny of the social institutions of the Victorian age. Students of *Hard Times* might read or dip into its immediate predecessor *Bleak House* (1853), which attacked the delays and incompetence of the law courts. The Smallweed family, who disregard the arts as a distraction from profitable business, can be compared with Gradgrind's point of view. Mr Chadband is an eloquent humbug. Anyone attracted by Dickens's style and **imagery** should read at least the first chapter of *Bleak House*. Dickens's interest in the building of the railways, which rapidly transformed England in the 1840s, can be seen in *Dombey and Son* (1848), and his concern with education in many novels, including the semi-autobiographical *David Copperfield* (1850). Time spent exploring Dickens's novels will invite many sorts of comparison, and could prove addictive.

HISTORICAL BACKGROUND

INDUSTRIAL BACKGROUND

Although *Hard Times* is not about a strike, and Coketown is a typical manufacturing town and not just a picture of Preston, the earliest readers were mindful of the cotton-weavers' strike at Preston, in its seventh month when the novel began to appear in *Household Words* in April 1854. 1848 had been a year of revolutions in Europe, and many people feared that the strike might spread and lead to a major social upheaval. Trade unions had only been legal for about thirty years; arguments between supporters of the union and friends of 'the Preston masters' (sarcastically called 'the cotton lords' by the strikers) influenced the social climate in which the novel was written.

Dickens visited Preston for a few days at the end of January 1854, and wrote an article, 'On Strike', for *Household Words* (see Part Six of this Note). He wrote of the orderly and dignified behaviour of the strikers, but he sympathised with both sides, and objected most to the idea that economic laws governing capital and labour, rather than moderation and good sense, must decide the outcome. 'On Strike' reports how one political economist laughed at him when he expressed this belief, insisting instead that the strikers must be crushed. Bounderby, with his hollow, blustery laughter, can be seen as Dickens's reply.

While he was in Preston Dickens attended a trade-union meeting and heard the so-called 'Thunderer of Lancashire', Mortimer Grimshaw, an aggressive and radical agitator and one of the leaders of the strike. He appears in 'On Strike' as 'Gruffshaw', and in *Hard Times* as Slackbridge. While Dickens admits that Gruffshaw was only one of the speakers and that his inflammatory speech was soon ended by the chairman, Slackbridge dominates the union meetings in *Hard Times*.

England was enjoying an economic boom in 1854. The title *Hard Times for these Times* refers to the conditions of life for factory workers, but challenges rather than reflects the mood of the country as a whole. The Great Exhibition in London in 1851 had shown that England led the world in technical and scientific progress. Thousands of new inventions, including powerful steam-engines, were on display. Steam contributed especially to the success of the Lancashire-based cotton industry. Any Lancastrian 'Gradgrind' would have come home inspired by the triumph of Fact. The novel, on the contrary, stresses the long hours, polluted environment and dangers from unshielded machinery endured by the factory workers who contributed to this prosperity.

Factory accidents

An article about factory accidents, accusing owners of negligence, was published in *Household Words* in 1854, while the novel was appearing there. This was 'Ground in the Mill' by Henry Morley, a piece commissioned and approved by Dickens (see Part Six of this Note). Morley describes horrific accidents to young people that could have been avoided, given proper safety measures. Dickens wrote but cancelled in proof an outspoken speech by Stephen about factory accidents, to have appeared in Book I Chapter 13 (see comments on the Summary in Part Two of this Note), perhaps to preserve the distinction between a novel and polemical journalism. Even so, reading of the 'crashing, smashing, tearing' factory machines (p. 73), and of the early death of Rachael's little sister, side by side with such articles, gave the earliest readers a sense of the novel's journalistic topicality and concern.

Education

The provision of schooling for all children was not achieved until after the Education Act of 1870, but many new schools were opened in the 1840s and 1850s. The 1840s saw the earliest teacher-training colleges. The difficulties facing reformers were enormous and the whole subject was controversial. Dickens was not alone in attacking overemphasis on memorising facts, in the training of teachers and in elementary schools. He particularly disliked the views of J.M. M'Culloch (1801–83), a Scottish reformer keen on facts and hostile to poetry in the classroom. M'Choakumchild, whose name may allude to M'Culloch's, has been trained together with 'some one hundred and forty other schoolmasters … lately turned at the same time, in the same factory, on the same principles, like so many pianoforte legs' (p. 15). The first batch of such trained teachers qualified in 1853. They faced huge classes of children of different ages all in the same barn-like rooms, so that numbering of pupils (as in 'girl number twenty') was often resorted to. Dickens feared that education would become dehumanised, and the novel's first two chapters give a nightmarish account of what things might be like at their worst.

The 'third gentleman' in this scene, who tells the children why horses should not be pictured on wallpaper, is often seen as a caricature of Henry Cole (1808–82), national director of art education in England from 1852. Cole was a strict **utilitarian**

Utilitarianism

Nineteenth-century English society was influenced in many ways by the writings of the **utilitarians**, Adam Smith (1723–90), the free-market economist, and Jeremy Bentham (1748–1832), whose rigorous argument for utility as the only social criterion led to reforms in law, government and education. Their principle of self-interest as the basis of all human action is **satirised** in *Hard Times*, especially in the person of Bitzer, who cites this view to Gradgrind in Book III Chapter 8. The doctrines of laissez-faire, or non-interference by government in commerce, advocated by followers of Adam Smith, and self-reliance, are satirised in Bounderby. Thomas Gradgrind has named two of his younger children after Adam Smith and Thomas Malthus (1766–1834), another utilitarian thinker best known for his views on population control.

Utilitarian ideas were responsible for necessary and valuable reforms, but were often applied without compassion for those involved. Bentham's ethical criterion of the greatest happiness of the greatest number led to misery, for example, in the Poor Law of 1834. The concept of measuring happiness in the mass, and the idea of average happiness, making individual suffering irrelevant, are satirised in Book I Chapter 9, 'Sissy's Progress'. The insensitivity of rigid utilitarians, including factory owners and their intellectual backers who declared compassion and sympathy to be meaningless, and narrow-minded educational reformers who stressed facts at the expense of imagination (see above, Education), provided Dickens with his targets. Above all, he hated, and attacked in Gradgrind, the complacency of utilitarians who quoted statistics, government reports, and economic laws, but disregarded the actual problems of people around them.

CIRCUSES

Dickens's article, 'The Amusements of the People', written for *Household Words* in 1850, shows his firm belief in popular entertainment, and defence of it against puritanical opponents. Many forms of popular entertainment, including traditional fairs and street theatres, were abolished or restricted in Dickens's lifetime. Sabbatarians objected to entertainments on Sunday. Teetotal societies objected to entertainments that encouraged drinking. Some hard-headed **utilitarians** objected to all entertainment, including theatre and literature, as meaningless nonsense. Dickens was passionately opposed to all such views.

The circus chapters are based on research by Dickens into currently popular acts, especially at Astley's Theatre in London. The modern reader needs to remember that Victorian circus entertainment overlapped with popular theatre, and included short pantomime acts, such as Babes in the Wood and Jack the Giant-killer, just as in Sleary's company. Fixed companies such as Astley's and travelling companies such as Sleary's in the novel offered a programme combining horse-riding acts, acrobatics and pantomime. A horse called the Flying Childers appeared at Astley's in 1853 and 1854, and perhaps gave Mr E.W.B. Childers his name. In

Book I Chapter 6, we read that 'the father of one of the families [in Sleary's troupe] was in the habit of balancing the father of another of the families on the top of a great pole' (p. 41). This act could be seen at three London theatres in 1853. Sleary resembles, in his lisp and vivacity, Jack Clark, a famous early nineteenth-century circus manager. For further reading on circuses, see Part Six of this Note.

DIVORCE

Divorce was a controversial subject in the mid 1850s. It provides an example of how **utilitarian** theory helped in causes supported by Dickens. Benthamite legal theory was influential in advocating that divorce law should be founded on utility rather than on religious precepts. A Royal Commission was appointed in 1850 to make a report. In 1853, the commissioners recommended moving matrimonial cases from religious to secular courts. A Divorce Act was eventually passed in 1857, abolishing Doctors' Commons (where Dickens had worked, 1830–32), the ecclesiastical court mentioned by Bounderby (p. 79). *Household Words* had contributed to the debate on divorce on the liberal side, complaining about the ridiculously high cost of obtaining a divorce under the old regulations.

LITERARY BACKGROUND

In his letter to Thomas Carlyle (1795–1881), asking permission to dedicate *Hard Times* to him, Dickens wrote, 'I do devoutly hope [it] will shake people in a terrible mistake of these days … I know it contains nothing in which you do not think with me, for no man knows your books better than I' (13 July 1854). Dickens revered Carlyle for a long series of polemical and historical books, including *Past and Present* (1843) and *Latter-Day Pamphlets* (1850). Dickens and Carlyle agreed in attacking social divisions and 'steam-engine philosophy' (Carlyle's phrase), by which they meant narrow and stupid forms of **utilitarianism**. Carlyle's writing inspired Dickens and may have helped give coherence to his ideas, although Dickens would probably have come to the same conclusions by himself. Carlyle had some influence on the prose style of

Hard Times, especially in the use of dramatic exclamations such as 'Utilitarian economists, skeletons of schoolmasters, Commissioners of Fact, genteel and used-up infidels, gabblers of many little dog's-eared creeds', all blamed and cursed together when Stephen leaves Coketown (p. 165).

Edward Bulwer-Lytton (1803–73), a prolific and very successful Victorian novelist whose work is neglected today, was one of Dickens's closest friends. Bulwer-Lytton's *England and the English* (1833), includes character sketches of Mr Bluff and Samuel Square. Mr Bluff is always stressing 'the facts'; he is practical and hates poets; he believes in the multiplication table. Mr Square is a new sort of radical who thinks men have no passions, but work like clockwork. He is a utilitarian and 'dry as a bone'. He lives by system and 'never feels for anyone'. Dickens may have had these portraits in the back of his mind when he conceived of Thomas Gradgrind.

Another close friend was the writer and editor John Forster (1812–76), Dickens's exact contemporary and first biographer (1872–4). He read all Dickens's novels in manuscript or proof. Dickens sent Forster a short-list of fourteen possible titles, and asked for his selections. Forster chose 'Hard Times', 'Prove It' and 'Simple Arithmetic'. Dickens had chosen 'Hard Times', 'A Mere Question of Figures', and 'The Gradgrind Philosophy'. 'Hard Times', their only joint selection, was adopted.

Elizabeth Gaskell (born Cleghorn 1810–65), a novelist who knew the north of England far better than Dickens, published *Mary Barton: A Tale of Manchester Life* in 1848, a story of industrial unrest. This book impressed Dickens, who invited her to contribute to *Household Words*, and later to *All the Year Round*. Her novel *North and South* followed *Hard Times* in *Household Words*. Dickens wrote to reassure her that their stories would not be too closely in competition, saying 'I have no intention of striking' (21 April 1854). Stephen and Rachael are sometimes compared unfavourably with Gaskell's realistic portrayal of northern working people.

Benjamin Disraeli (1804–81), novelist and politician, also dealt with social problems, notably in *Sybil: or, The Two Nations* (1845). His demonstration, in the words of this novel, that England had become two nations, 'the rich and the poor', defines the problem with which much of Dickens's later work is concerned.

PART SIX

CRITICAL HISTORY & BROADER PERSPECTIVES

NINETEENTH-CENTURY VIEWS

Nineteenth-century critics tended to acknowledge Dickens's genius but deplore his faults. Some of the fault-finding was upper-class disapproval: Dickens was 'low' and vulgar, and did not know about gentlemen. Some critics regretted his use of sentimentality and **melodrama** to reach a wide readership. A constant complaint was exaggeration, provoking the philosopher George Santayana (1863–1952), who shared Dickens's sense of the grotesqueness of life, to say that people who thought the novels exaggerated must have 'no eyes and no ears', but only 'notions of what things and people are like'. Even his harshest critics admitted he was a comic and imaginative writer of the highest order.

Nineteenth-century criticism of *Hard Times* was divided, for and against. John Ruskin (1819–1900), revered as a critic of art and society, offered a memorable short verdict:

> Allowing for his manner of telling them, the things he tells us are always true. I wish that he could think it right to limit his brilliant exaggeration to works written only for public amusement; and when he takes up a subject of high national importance, such as that which he handled in *Hard Times*, that he would use severer and more accurate analysis ... But let us not lose the use of Dickens's wit and insight because he chooses to speak in a circle of stage fire ... all [his books] but especially *Hard Times*, should be studied with close and earnest care by persons interested in social questions ... [who will find] that his view was finally the right one, grossly and sharply told.

This 'Note on Hard Times' from Ruskin's *Unto this Last* (1862) is reprinted in full in the Norton Critical Edition, edited by George Ford and Sylvère Monod (Norton, New York & London, 1990), p. 332, where a useful selection of historical materials, extracts from Dickens's notes and plans for the novel, and critical essays, can be found. Dickens's articles 'On Strike' and 'The Amusements of the People' can be found here, as can Morley's 'Ground in the Mill', mentioned above. George Santayana's defence of Dickens against the charge of exaggeration, from *Soliloquies in England* (1922), is reprinted in Stephen Wall's excellent critical anthology, *Charles Dickens* (Penguin, 1970).

SOCIALIST VIEWS

The dramatist George Bernard Shaw (1856–1950) wrote an introduction to *Hard Times* in 1912. Shaw praised the novel as a denunciation of 'our entire social system', a rejection of any possibility of limited reform, and so, whether Dickens was fully conscious of it or not, a call for the transformation of society. Shaw warned that 'England is full of Bounderbys ... and Gradgrinds; and we are all to a quite appalling extent in their power'. Unlike several critics who complain of a lack of normal Dickensian amusement, Shaw said that in this novel Dickens 'casts off for ever all restraint on his wild sense of humour'. Shaw compares Dickens to a mad clown 'in a very mad harlequinade', conveying truths about human behaviour through grotesquely presented characters, and picks out Mrs Sparsit for special praise. The one part of the book Shaw objects to is Slackbridge and the union; he asserts that Dickens had no idea what Victorian trade unions were like. This lively, stimulating essay is reprinted in the Norton Critical Edition (quotations, pp. 336–7).

Another influential critic with a socialist approach was Raymond Williams (b.1921). Williams admires Bounderby, seeing in him 'the embodiment of the aggressive money-making and power-seeking ideal which was a driving force of the Industrial Revolution'. His difficulty comes with Gradgrind, since 'the case against him is so good, and his refutation by experience so masterly, that it is easy for the modern reader to forget what Gradgrind is'. He is the very type of the Victorian reformer. In condemning him, the reader is asked 'to condemn the kind of thinking and the methods of enquiry and legislation which in fact promoted a large measure of social and industrial reform'. The 'methods of enquiry' means the patient gathering and tabulating of statistics, on which Dickens pours scorn throughout. Legislation, which did produce factory acts and education acts, came about in the House of Commons, conscientiously attended by Gradgrind, which Dickens condemns as a dung heap.

Williams goes on to charge Dickens with having no political position. He merely 'defends individuals and persons against the system'. For Dickens, Williams says, exploitation and reform are 'two sides to the same coin, Industrialism'. His rejection of both is 'adolescent'. Given Williams's point of view (it is almost like hearing the early Gradgrind answering Dickens back), this is a rigorous argument. Williams concludes: '*Hard Times* is more a symptom of the confusion of industrial society than an understanding of it, but it is a symptom that is significant and continuing.' This discussion is from Williams's *Culture and Society, 1780–1950* (Chatto & Windus, 1958, pp. 92–7).

HARD TIMES AS A WORK OF ART

The combative, Cambridge-based critic F.R. Leavis (1895–1978) argued in favour of the novel as an artistic, 'poetic' masterpiece, in his controversial and influential book on English fiction, *The Great Tradition* (Chatto & Windus, 1948). Leavis gives a clear account of the circus as a symbol of 'vital human needs' denied by Gradgrind and Bounderby. He writes well about the representative significance of the characters, and brings out how it is that Gradgrind's love for his children is thwarted by his misrepresenting it to himself as love for his 'system'. Leavis singles out *Hard Times* in *The Great Tradition* as the only novel by Dickens worth serious attention, but amply amends this judgement later in *Dickens the Novelist*, written jointly with his wife Q.D. Leavis (Chatto & Windus, 1970).

Leavis's praise for *Hard Times* drew increased critical attention to the novel in the following decades. Robert Garis aimed to replace Leavis's idea of Dickens as a poetic symbolist with the concept of 'a theatrical artist', one who makes us aware of his *performance* of the roles of characters and narrator, and aware too of his pleasure in manipulating language. It is not, Garis says, Gradgrind or Bounderby or the narrator that we enjoy, but Dickens being Gradgrind or Bounderby or the story-teller, making them dramatise themselves. Many Dickensians find Garis persuasive. He can also make us wonder how far Dickens's art served his social criticism and how far social criticism served his art. There is a chapter on *Hard Times* in Robert Garis, *The Dickens Theatre: A Reassessment of the Novels* (Clarendon Press, Oxford, 1965).

Other outstanding essays include John Holloways's '*Hard Times*: a History and a Criticism', in John Gross and Gabriel Pearson (eds), *Dickens and the Twentieth Century* (Routledge and Kegan Paul, 1962), and Juliet McMaster's account of colour imagery in her *Dickens the Designer* (Macmillan, 1983; reprinted in Norton).

POLYPHONY

Roger Fowler uses the concept of polyphony (many voices), introduced by the Russian critic Mikhail Bakhtin, in his discussion of contrasts of speech style. He examines Sleary and Slackbridge as 'linguistic grotesques'. Each has an idiolect or individual style of speech, and they contribute to the 'polyphonic structure' of competing voices. Sleary's slurred speech makes us concentrate on his words, which challenge the emphatic speeches of Gradgrind. There are also sociolects, or social dialects. Some of Sleary's speech habits link him with working-class dialect-speakers such as Stephen, whereas Slackbridge, who has no dialect features, uses formulas derived from radical political pamphlets. Stephen's style of speaking contrasts with Bounderby's bullying style, which is 'packed with demands and commands'. Fowler's work combines Bakhtin's speech styles with M.A.K. Halliday's 'functional' theory of language, which analyses registers, or linguistic varieties reflecting different views of the world within one community. This careful study first appeared in R. Giddings (ed.), *The Changing World of Charles Dickens* (Vision Press, 1983), and has often been reprinted.

DECONSTRUCTION

Steven Connor is a deconstructive critic, seeking to find 'internal dissention' or 'warring forces of signification' in Dickens's novels, while disregarding traditional interpretations of the author's intentions. He takes *Hard Times* to be 'a test case' for deconstruction because the author's intentions seem to be so clear.

Beginning with the linguistic distinction between metonymy and metaphor, Connor ingeniously associates Fact with metaphor and Fancy with metonymy. Gradgrindery is marked by 'metaphorical fixing'. Gradgrind's square head and square house signify Gradgrind. The bits of

Bounderby's front door, such as the letters on his name plate, signify Bounderby. The circus, on the other hand, is marked by 'metonymic deferral'. The description of the Pegasus's Arms is full of details, one leading to another.

This is surprising, as Connor says. We would have expected the opposite because Dickens's style is so metaphorical. Connor declares that 'metaphor is used to discredit metaphor as Dickens mounts a systematic assault on systematic thought' (p. 97). Connor's analysis requires us to look very closely at the passages he selects, and to consider how consistently Dickens uses the distinction between fact and fancy, and whether interpretations that rely exclusively on this opposition make sense (for a different view, see Themes, on Fancy).

Not all readers will be persuaded that the novel is about its own incoherence, however. Some may feel that Dickens's target is not systematic thought, but obsession with it, and the kind of intellectual complacency that blinds its exponents to the human suffering which is the novel's subject.

Steven Connor's chapter on *Hard Times* is in his *Charles Dickens* (Oxford University Press, 1985).

FEMINIST CRITICISM

Jean Ferguson Carr's essay 'Writing as a Woman: Dickens, *Hard Times* and Feminine Discourses' begins by discussing a renowned attack on Dickens by the Victorian critic G.H. Lewes (1817–78). Lewes associated Dickens with women writers, who, he says, set emotion over rationality. Carr maintains that feminine discourse in the nineteenth century threatened the **patriarchal** literary and social order that Lewes wanted to maintain. In grouping Dickens with women writers who 'overemphasised' feeling and fancy, Lewes can be said to have perceived him to be 'writing as a woman'. Modern critics who deplore Dickens's sentimentality perpetuate the stereotype of a weak, unmanly side to Dickens. In *Hard Times*, Carr argues, the idea of 'fancy', and the word itself (rather than 'imagination'), belong to the feminine element in Victorian culture, as men such as Lewes conceived it, and perhaps still do.

Carr goes on to discuss how women in the story are silenced by the powerful male discourse of the Gradgrind system. Gradgrindery, she says, exploits the patriarchal authority summed up by Mikhail Bakhtin (see above, Polyphony) as 'the word of the fathers' – never to be disputed. Under this rule, Mrs Gradgrind has become a shadowy figure, unable to fulfil her role as a Victorian mother. Louisa is like her mother in being unable to find words for her situation, especially in the scene with her father where she has almost nothing to say about marrying Bounderby. Even Sissy, who is so impressive in her scene with Harthouse, opposes him best by not arguing with him.

Although Dickens was 'a powerful male writer', therefore, his empathy with women in the excluded and silenced place accorded them under the male rule of Fact enabled him to disturb, although not to challenge openly, the patriarchal culture of his time.

This brief summary conveys little of the subtlety and close reasoning of Jean Ferguson Carr's essay, which needs to be read entire. First published in *Dickens Studies Annual*, 18 (1989), it is reprinted in Stephen Connor (ed.), *Charles Dickens* (Longman, 1996, pp. 159–177).

Students interested in Dickens's treatment of women might consult Michael Slater's *Dickens and Women* (Deutsch, 1983). Slater argues that Dickens became concerned with women as the 'insulted and injured of mid-Victorian England' during the years 1847 to 1857, and gave female characters more prominent roles in his novels of this period (pp. 243–4).

FURTHER READING

Margaret Simpson's *The Companion to Hard Times*, Helm Information, Mountfield, East Sussex, 1997, is full of detailed information on every aspect of the novel, and has a full bibliography. The chapter on *Hard Times* in John Butt and Kathleen Tillotson, *Dickens at Work*, Methuen, 1957, examines the problems of weekly serialisation. Those interested in Victorian circuses and popular entertainment should consult Paul Schlicke, *Dickens and Popular Entertainment*, George Allen & Unwin, 1985, which includes a chapter on entertainment in *Hard Times*.

Historical events	Dickens's life	Cultural events
		1811 William Makepeace Thackeray born
1812 Napoleon's retreat from Moscow	**1812** Charles John Huffam Dickens born Portsmouth	
		1813 Jane Austen, *Sense and Sensibility*
1815 Battle of Waterloo		
	1816 Family moves to Chatham	
		1818 Mary Shelley, *Frankenstein*
		1819 'George Eliot' born
1820 Death of George III; first gas lighting in cities		
		1821 John Keats dies; Feodor Dostoevski born
	1822 Family moves to London	
1824 Trade Unions officially allowed	**1824** Father imprisoned for debt; Dickens works in shoe-blacking factory	
	1824-7 At school at Wellington House Academy	
1825 First railway Stockton-Darlington		
1826 First Atlantic crossing under steam		
		1827 William Blake dies, Beethoven dies
	1829 Falls in love with Maria Beadnell	
		1831 Victor Hugo, *The Hunchback of Notre-Dame*
1832 Reform Bill passed	**1832** Becomes reporter of debates in House of Commons	**1832** Walter Scott dies; Goethe dies; Jeremy Bentham dies
		1832-4 Harriet Martineau, *Illustrations of Political Economy*
1833 First British Factory Act		
1834 Tolpuddle Martyrs; first electric light	**1834** Becomes reporter on *Morning Chronicle*	

Historical events	Dickens's life	Cultural events
1836 People's Charter	**1836** Meets John Forster, friend, adviser and biographer	
	1836-7 *Sketches by Boz; The Posthumous Papers of the Pickwick Club;* marries Catherine Hogarth	
1837 Accession of Queen Victoria	**1837-8** *Oliver Twist*	
1838 First photographic prints	**1838-9** *Nicholas Nickleby*	
1839 First electric telegraph in use on railways		
	1840-1 *The Old Curiosity Shop*	**1840** Thomas Hardy and Emile Zola born
1841 London-Bristol railway opened; hundreds of new railway lines constructed during next decade	**1841** *Barnaby Rudge*	
	1842 Visits America	
	1843-4 *Martin Chuzzlewit*	**1843** Thomas Carlyle's *Past and Present* attacks laissez-faire economics and arouses sympathy for industrial poor
	1844 Visits Italy	
	1845 *A Christmas Carol*	
	1846 Founds *Daily News;* visits Switzerland	
1847 Burdett-Coutts founds home for Homeless Women	**1847** Helps set up home for Homeless Women	**1847** Emily Brontë, *Wuthering Heights;* Charlotte Brontë, *Jane Eyre;* Anne Brontë, *Agnes Grey*
1848 Revolutions in Paris, Berlin, Vienna, Venice, Rome, Milan, Prague and Budapest	**1848** *Dombey and Son*	**1848** Elizabeth Gaskell, *Mary Barton;* Thackeray, *Vanity Fair;* Karl Marx, *Communist Manifesto*
	1849-50 *David Copperfield*	
1850 First refrigerator	**1850** Starts *Household Words*	**1850** Guy de Maupassant born; Tennyson becomes Poet Laureate; Nathaniel Hawthorne, *The Scarlet Letter;* Wordsworth and Balzac die
	1850-2 *Bleak House*	

Historical events	Dickens's life	Cultural events
1851 Great Exhibition; gold discovered in Australia		**1851** The painter Turner dies; Henry Mayhew, *London Labour and London Poor;* Herman Melville, *Moby Dick*
1852 First airship		
1853 Chloroform given medical approval		
1853-4 Cotton worker's strike, Preston		
1853-6 Crimean War		
	1854 Visits Preston; *Hard Times*	
	1855-7 *Little Dorrit*	**1855** Elizabeth Gaskell, *North and South;* Charlotte Brontë dies
1857 Indian Mutiny		**1857** Gustave Flaubert, *Madame Bovary*
	1858 Separates from wife; in love with Ellen Ternan	
	1859 *A Tale of Two Cities*	**1859** Charles Darwin, *On the Origin of Species;* George Eliot, *Adam Bede*
	1860 Moves to Gad's Hill, near Rochester	
	1860-1 *Great Expectations*	
1861 First telephone		
		1862 Victor Hugo, *Les Misérables*
	1863 Son Walter dies in India	**1863** Thackeray dies; Charles Kingsley, *The Water-Babies*
	1864-5 *Our Mutual Friend*	
	1867-8 Revisits America	
1868 First bicycle (bone-shaker)		
		1869 Leo Tolstoy, *War and Peace*
1870 Education Act; all children to have elementary education	**1870** Dies; *The Mystery of Edwin Drood* unfinished	
		1871-2 George Eliot, *Middlemarch*
	1872-4 John Forster's *Life of Dickens*	

allegory a story to be read in two or more ways; the names of people and places are sometimes clues: in *Pilgrim's Progress*, the hero Christian leaves the City of Destruction and begins a journey to salvation

apostrophise an apostrophe is a speech addressed to someone or something

blank verse unrhymed iambic pentameter (ti-tum ti-tum ti-tum ti-tum ti-tum: 'Oh good Horatio, what a wounded name'), the commonest English verse metre; Dickens sometimes falls into a rhythm close to this, in heightened passages

chorus in classical drama, a group of characters who comment on the action

closure the sense of an ending, happy, tragic or thoughtful, which marks the end of a story or play; deliberately unfinished or unresolved stories are sometimes said to be 'open-ended'

deconstruction deconstructive criticism aims to show the incoherence held to be inevitable in any text, given the indeterminate nature of meaning

dramatic irony occurs when a play's audience or readers of a story know or guess more about the situation than the characters do

epithet a descriptive word or phrase added to a person's name

fable short tale, or narrative pattern in a novel, conveying a clear moral lesson

feminism a doctrine that advocates equal rights for women; see also patriarchy

idiolect the linguistic peculiarities of an individual speaker

imagery, image (i) a picture created by words, as in 'the image of Louisa sitting by the fire' (ii) a metaphor or a simile, as in 'like the head of an elephant'. Recurring imagery can create patterns in a story

irony saying one thing and meaning another; understatement is one form; another states what ought to be but is not the case

melodrama a sensational story with unlikely events and unrealistic dialogue

metaphor a figure of speech in which one thing is described as being another thing, which in a simile it would only have been compared to

metonymy a figure of speech where a part stands for the whole: a 'Hand' for a workman. Metonymy can be seen as one fundamental mode of language and metaphor as the other. The bits and pieces of the world jostle together: streams of smoke, chimneys, steam-engines. Metaphor pictures a steam engine as an elephant's head

omniscient narrator a story-teller who has a godlike knowledge of events and of thoughts and feelings in the minds of the characters; see point of view

patriarchy originally, rule by the fathers (of a tribe or village). In feminist criticism refers to ways in which culture is organised according to masculine values

personification a figure of speech treating things or ideas as if they were human, as in 'Time, the great manufacturer'

point of view a story can be told by one of the characters, or from another point of view. The point of view can change from one part of the story to another when events are viewed through the minds of two or more characters; see omniscient narrator

polyphony coexistence of many voices, or many points of view, not subjected to or controlled by a single authorial voice

rhetoric rhetorical devices, such as repetition, in Bounderby's speeches and in passages of commentary in *Hard Times*, belong to rhetoric, the art of using language persuasively

rhetorical question an assertion made in the form of a question to which the answer is assumed to be obvious

satire literature that shows or examines vice and folly and makes them appear ridiculous or contemptible

sociolect social dialect

symbol something that represents something else (often an abstract idea) by association or convention, for example 'the heart' often symbolises the emotions

utilitarian (a philosophical term) making utility and the benefit or happiness of the greatest number of people, rather than religion or tradition, the criteria for ethical and social practice; it is the view of life underlying most modern political and economic thought. Dickens satirised abuses of utilitarian theory (including overemphasis on fact, and disregard for individual hardship), but also disliked the assumption that human happiness can be politically measured or controlled

Neil McEwan read English at Pembroke College, Oxford, and teaches in the English Department at Nara Women's University, Japan. He has published several critical studies, including *The Survival of the Novel* (Macmillan, 1981), *Africa and the Novel* (Macmillan, 1983), *Perspective in British Historical Fiction Today* (Macmillan, 1987), and *Graham Greene* (1988) and *Anthony Powell* (1991) in the 'Macmillan Modern Novelists' series. He edited Volume 5, *The Twentieth Century*, in *The Macmillan Anthologies of English Literature* (1989). He is the author of *Preparing for Examinations in English Literature*, in York Handbooks, and *Alice Walker: The Color Purple*, in York Notes Advanced.

Notes

York Notes Advanced

Margaret Atwood
The Handmaid's Tale

Jane Austen
Mansfield Park

Jane Austen
Persuasion

Jane Austen
Pride and Prejudice

Alan Bennett
Talking Heads

William Blake
Songs of Innocence and of Experience

Charlotte Brontë
Jane Eyre

Emily Brontë
Wuthering Heights

Geoffrey Chaucer
The Franklin's Tale

Geoffrey Chaucer
General Prologue to the Canterbury Tales

Geoffrey Chaucer
The Wife of Bath's Prologue and Tale

Joseph Conrad
Heart of Darkness

Charles Dickens
Great Expectations

John Donne
Selected Poems

George Eliot
The Mill on the Floss

F. Scott Fitzgerald
The Great Gatsby

E.M. Forster
A Passage to India

Brian Friel
Translations

Thomas Hardy
The Mayor of Casterbridge

Thomas Hardy
Tess of the d'Urbervilles

Seamus Heaney
Selected Poems from Opened Ground

Nathaniel Hawthorne
The Scarlet Letter

James Joyce
Dubliners

John Keats
Selected Poems

Christopher Marlowe
Doctor Faustus

Arthur Miller
Death of a Salesman

Toni Morrison
Beloved

William Shakespeare
Antony and Cleopatra

William Shakespeare
As You Like It

William Shakespeare
Hamlet

William Shakespeare
King Lear

William Shakespeare
Measure for Measure

William Shakespeare
The Merchant of Venice

William Shakespeare
Much Ado About Nothing

William Shakespeare
Othello

William Shakespeare
Romeo and Juliet

William Shakespeare
The Tempest

William Shakespeare
The Winter's Tale

Mary Shelley
Frankenstein

Alice Walker
The Color Purple

Oscar Wilde
The Importance of Being Earnest

Tennessee Williams
A Streetcar Named Desire

John Webster
The Duchess of Malfi

W.B. Yeats
Selected Poems

GCSE and equivalent levels

Maya Angelou
I Know Why the Caged Bird Sings

Jane Austen
Pride and Prejudice

Alan Ayckbourn
Absent Friends

Elizabeth Barrett Browning
Selected Poems

Robert Bolt
A Man for All Seasons

Harold Brighouse
Hobson's Choice

Charlotte Brontë
Jane Eyre

Emily Brontë
Wuthering Heights

Shelagh Delaney
A Taste of Honey

Charles Dickens
David Copperfield

Charles Dickens
Great Expectations

Charles Dickens
Hard Times

Charles Dickens
Oliver Twist

Roddy Doyle
Paddy Clarke Ha Ha Ha

George Eliot
Silas Marner

George Eliot
The Mill on the Floss

William Golding
Lord of the Flies

Oliver Goldsmith
She Stoops To Conquer

Willis Hall
The Long and the Short and the Tall

Thomas Hardy
Far from the Madding Crowd

Thomas Hardy
The Mayor of Casterbridge

Thomas Hardy
Tess of the d'Urbervilles

Thomas Hardy
The Withered Arm and other Wessex Tales

L.P. Hartley
The Go-Between

Seamus Heaney
Selected Poems

Susan Hill
I'm the King of the Castle

Barry Hines
A Kestrel for a Knave

Louise Lawrence
Children of the Dust

Harper Lee
To Kill a Mockingbird

Laurie Lee
Cider with Rosie

Arthur Miller
The Crucible

Arthur Miller
A View from the Bridge

Robert O'Brien
Z for Zachariah

Frank O'Connor
My Oedipus Complex and other stories

George Orwell
Animal Farm

J.B. Priestley
An Inspector Calls

Willy Russell
Educating Rita

Willy Russell
Our Day Out

J.D. Salinger
The Catcher in the Rye

William Shakespeare
Henry IV Part 1

William Shakespeare
Henry V

William Shakespeare
Julius Caesar

William Shakespeare
Macbeth

William Shakespeare
The Merchant of Venice

William Shakespeare
A Midsummer Night's Dream

William Shakespeare
Much Ado About Nothing

William Shakespeare
Romeo and Juliet

William Shakespeare
The Tempest

William Shakespeare
Twelfth Night

George Bernard Shaw
Pygmalion

Mary Shelley
Frankenstein

R.C. Sherriff
Journey's End

Rukshana Smith
Salt on the snow

John Steinbeck
Of Mice and Men

Robert Louis Stevenson
Dr Jekyll and Mr Hyde

Jonathan Swift
Gulliver's Travels

Robert Swindells
Daz 4 Zoe

Mildred D. Taylor
Roll of Thunder, Hear My Cry

Mark Twain
Huckleberry Finn

James Watson
Talking in Whispers

William Wordsworth
Selected Poems

A Choice of Poets

Mystery Stories of the Nineteenth Century including The Signalman

Nineteenth Century Short Stories

Poetry of the First World War

Six Women Poets